JOB

THE SOVEREIGNTY OF GOD

AND THE SUFFERING OF MAN

by

Cyril J. Barber

WIPF & STOCK · Eugene, Oregon

JOB
The Sovereignty of God and the Suffering of Man

Wipf & Stock
An imprint of Wipf and Stock Publishers
199 W. 8th Avenue, Suite 3
Eugene OR, 97401
www.wipfandstock.com

ISBN 13: 978-1-62564-489-3

Manufactured in the U.S.A.

The Author

Cyril Barber, D.Litt., D.Min., D.D., spent 25 years as an educator in Christian colleges and universities and a further 25+ years in pastoral ministry. Now "retired" he spends his time writing. He lives with Aldyth his wife of more than fifty-five years in Hacienda Heights, California. Their family consists of two sons, two daughters-in-law, five grandchildren, and three great grandchildren.

CONTENTS

GOD'S REVELATION

PROLOGUE

We are deeply grateful to translators of the book of Job (particularly those involved in the production of the *New American Standard Bible*) for providing a clear, accurate and readable translation of the book of Job. Also of value are the translations of the *New International Version*, and the *New English Bible*. To avoid the charge of plagiarism I have provided my own translation of key passages, but my faltering attempt to bring out the meaning of the original Hebrew falls far short of the contribution of scholars who produced the *NASB*, *NIV,* and *NEB*

At the outset it must be pointed out that the contents of this monograph were not written for the scholar. From first to last it has been designed for lay people who desire to come to grips with the teaching of this portion of God's Word (cf. 2 Timothy 3:16). During the early 1960s I had the privilege of studying under the late Dr. Merrill F. Unger, and I have made extensive use of his *Commentary on the Old Testament* (published by AMG, Chattanooga, TN37421).

The book of Job deals with the weighty issues of God's sovereignty, Satan's malevolent opposition, and the problems that accompany unexplained human suffering. Included in the Bible are principles that will help us cope with the trials and difficulties we all face, for Job was not a fictitious character, but a real flesh-and-blood human being like us. To the best of his ability he maintained a relationship with the Lord, and his experiences provide hope for us when we are called upon to suffer.

Of course, there are those who claim that Job was not a real person, but the Old Testament prophet Ezekiel spoke of him as a historical figure (Ezekiel 14:14, 20), and James, the brother of the Lord Jesus, did the same (James 5:11). The apostle Paul twice quoted from the book that bears Job's name (Romans 11:35; 1 Corinthians 3:19), and he authenticated the historicity of Job's trials and perturbation. This leaves no doubt that Job was a real person, not a mythical character.

But why do the righteous suffer? Most would-be helpers align themselves with Job's "comforters" and claim that all suffering is the result of sin (cf. John 9:2). Theologians debate the issues within the scope of God's sovereignty. They claim that sometimes ill-health or the capricious reverses of nature are allowed by God to test us. And behind the scenes is our ever-vigilant enemy, Satan, who is always ready to turn us from the path of righteousness (cf. Zechariah 3:1*b*).

Peter may have had the experiences of Job in mind when he pointed out that God is honored when the righteous suffer patiently (1 Peter 2:20*b*).

In closing I would like to thank those who have stood by me and been a constant source of encouragement throughout the difficulties of a writing ministry: My wife Aldyth; Maurice Bickley and David Cahn who have worked tirelessly in preparing the MS for publication; and Robert Krauss, librarian *par excellence*, Biola University. Their help and assistance has been of great encouragement to me. To all I say a very sincere "Thank you!"

CHAPTER ONE

WHO WAS JOB?[1]

During our last year in Canada a tragic accident rocked the church. A devout couple, who were "pillars" in the assembly, lost their youngest son. This couple's two older sons and daughter were married, while their third son, the youngest, was still in college. On this particular Sunday afternoon he went outside to wash the family car, which he was scheduled to use that evening when he took his girl-friend to a youth meeting.

This lad's mother and father were in the house where they were relaxing after having washed and put away the dinner dishes. All of a sudden there was a screeching of tires followed by a thud, and then the sound of a car hurry-ing away.

Suspecting the worst the couple rushed outside where their fears were confirmed. On the street a yard from the car lay the youngest member of their family. His body showed no signs of life. His father hastened inside and called 911, while his wife held her son in her arms. An ambulance came, but the young man was pronounced dead at the scene.

---

1. Is all we know about Job confined to the New Testament statement made by James where he spoke of the sufferings of Job and the outcome of the Lord's dealings with him (James 5:11)? Fortunately for us, much more is revealed about him in the Old Testament book that bears his name and in a few other references (e.g., Ezekiel 14:14, 20).

His parents were crushed by this sudden calamity, and his mother kept asking, "How could God do this to us? If God is a God of love, why would He allow this tragedy to take from us the son whom we dearly love? And if He is all-powerful, why didn't He prevent our son's death?"

The grieving father also could not understand why the Lord would allow such a tragedy. His wife, however, conceived of their loss as punishment; but for what? What had they done wrong that would cause Him to inflict such pain upon them? It wasn't long before her frustration over her unanswered questions turned to anger. In an endeavor to weigh their good works on a scale she began thinking of all the good she and her husband had done. They served on church committees, taught in the Sunday school, and gave liberally to missions. What more could be required of them?

Her feeling of anger made it easy for her to conclude that God had dealt unjustly with them. She stopped going to the midweek Bible study group, and soon stopped going to church. On one occasion some close friends heard her say, "I'll never pray to God again. I cannot pray to someone who is so heartless and vindictive that he would snatch my son from me."

It took time, but the husband and father grew through his grief. His wife, however, remained stubborn; she clung to her resentment against God, and even turned away from all who tried to console her.

When we left Canada, and later Illinois, to take a position on the faculty of a graduate school in California, we kept in touch with our friends. From them we learned that even the passing of the years failed to soften this mother's heart; and in spite of numerous prayers on her behalf she had clung to her belief that God had dealt unjustly with her.

Years before this woman's son was killed, a songwriter wrote:

Judge not the Lord by feeble sense,
But trust Him for His grace;
Behind a frowning Providence
He hides a smiling face.

Blind unbelief is sure to err,
And scan God's work in vain;
God is His own interpreter,
And He will make it plain.[2]

This dear woman's grief over her loss is not unusual. In our modern world, with its technological mentality, we are obsessed with the need to be in complete control of our lives. We believe that the world is something we can understand and regulate, and we tend to see life in terms of questions which we can answer.

---

2. H. S. Milford, ed., *The Poetical Works of William Cowper* (London: Oxford University Press, 1963), 455.

But where can we go to find answers to the question of life and death, suffering and our conflicting emotions? One of the lessons that emerges from a careful reading of the book of Job is that God is sovereign and sometimes allows us to walk through the "valley of the shadow" because there is no other way for us to discover His far-reaching plan and purpose for us. Job illustrates the process through which he passed, and along the way the book that bears his name shows us how we can handle what we perceive to be the grave inequities of life. Once we have experienced what has been called the "dark night of the soul" we become stronger and better able to help others.[3]

When Did Job Live?

Job lived *before* the lifetime of Abraham, probably around 2200 B.C. Evidence for this comes from the patriarchal period. It shows Job to have extensive livestock and great wealth; it also testifies to the fact that he served regularly as the family's priest by offering sacrifices for his family. And then there is Job's great age at the time of his death (cf. Job 42:16), that fits in with the patriarchal age. And there is no mention of Abraham or the establishment of

3. At no time should we ignore the teaching of Scripture concerning grief. The Apostle Paul wrote: "Blessed be the God and Father of our Lord Jesus Christ, the Father of mercies and God of all comfort, who comforts us in all our affliction so that we will be able to comfort those who are in any affliction with the comfort with which we ourselves are comforted by God" (2 Corinthians 1:3-5, NASB).

Israel as a nation, or the giving of the Law. All this points to an era before the time of Abraham and the other patriarchs.

Where Did Job Live?

But where did Job live? The Bible tells us that he lived in the land of Uz. But where was Uz? Evidence from Lamentations 4:21 indicates an area south and east of the Dead Sea, for Uz is later referred to as the land of Edom.[4]

The position of Uz may further be deduced from the residences of Job's friends: Eliphaz, the Temanite, was an Edomite; Elihu, the Buzite, was possibly a neighbor of the Chaldeans; and Bildad, the Shuhite, was one of the Bene-Kedem.[5] The land of Uz is also mentioned by Jeremiah (see Jeremiah 25:20) and is grouped with Egypt, Philistia, Edom, and Moab.

Who Wrote the Story of Job's Trials?

An earlier generation of biblical scholars attempted to see in the story of Job a compilation of Akkadian myths and legends. These views probably had their origin in Babylon

---

4. A contrary view to the one presented here comes from the eminent Bible scholar, Merrill F. Unger, whose writings are of the utmost value. See his *Unger's Commentary on the Old Testament.* 2 vols in 1 (Chattanooga, TN: AMG, 2002), 679.
5. Bildad lived in an area adjacent to Edom that was later inhabited by the descendants of Shuah, one of Abraham's sons by his wife Keturah (Genesis 25:1-2).

during the second half of the second millennium B.C., and were later taken over by the Akkadians. Recent translators have given two of them the titles, "Man and His God," and "I will praise the Lord of Wisdom." They treat the suffering of pious individuals who recognized their helplessness before their god. They were later shown mercy and restored to health and happiness.[6]

These myths bear a certain similarity to the experiences of Job, but their internal evidence reveals them to be of a totally different genre.

Other writers attributed the compilation of the book of Job to the Exilic Period of Israel's history (though this is unlikely, for Ezekiel [14:14] mentions the patriarch in the past tense). Still others are of the opinion that Job was written by scholars living in the Solomonic Age (950 B.C.); and still others hold to the Mosaic authorship.

Moses is the most likely author, for he lived closer to the time of the patriarchs than any of the others, pastored his father-in-law's sheep in roughly the same area, and was thoroughly familiar with the customs of the people and events of the period. He was also trained in all the wisdom of Egypt, and his literary gifts are readily evident in his writings, and especially his songs (cf. Exodus 15:1-21 and Deuteronomy 31:30–32:47).

---

6. J. B. Pritchard, ed., *The Ancient Near East: Supplementary Texts Relating to the Old Testament* (Princeton, NJ: Princeton University Press, 1969), 160ff., and 596ff.

An Outline of the Book of Job

The book of Job may be outlined as follows:

Prologue, 1:1–2:13
- Job's Family and His Faithfulness, 1:1-5
- Job's Unexpected Calamities, 1:6-2:10
- Job's Friends, 2:11-13

Job's Discussions With His Friends, 3:1–31:40
- Job's Lamentation, 3:1-26
- The First Round, 4:1–14:23
- The Second Round, 15:1–21:34
- Thee Third Round, 22:1–26:14
- Job's Final Response, 27:1–31:40

The Words of Elihu, 32:1–37:24

The Vindication of the Lord, 38:1–42:6
- The First Round, 38:1–40:5
- The Second Round, 40:6–42:6

Epilogue, 42:7-17

A careful consideration of the book of Job reveals a host of unexpected riches. These include insights into God's sovereignty, and His goodness and justice; Satan is shown to be the adversary of God and the accuser of His people (cf. Zechariah 3:1; Revelation 12:9-10); and Job illustrates for us the appropriate response of a sufferer to his suffering.[7]

We also learn from Job's rebuke of his "comforters" that all suffering is not the result of sin. Eliphaz took as the basis of his authority his experience that included a supposed vision of a spirit that visited him in the night. Bildad was less sensitive than Eliphaz and claimed that the death of Job's children was due to their sins. The basis of his authority was tradition. Zophar was the harshest of the three and claimed intuition as the basis of his world view.

Finally Elihu, the youngest of Job's "friends," apparently having witnessed the entire confrontation, when he could restrain himself no longer, chided Job for his stubbornness and rebuked him for charging God with hostility toward him.

All of Job's visitors asserted that suffering was due to sin; and, if we are honest with ourselves, we have to admit that, though we have refined our understanding of the cause of our hardship and suffering, we have not advanced much beyond these early philosophers.

What May We Expect From our Study of the Book of Job?

The highly respected Australian theologian and Research Fellow in the Australian Institute of Archaeology, Dr. Francis I. Anderson, has provided us with a most important commentary on the Book of Job. In his Introduc-

7. For an explanation of the process of grief and how it may be healed, see *Through the Valley of Tears* (Eugene, OR: Wipf and Stock, 1981), 216pp.

tion he wrote, "Men seek an explanation of suffering in cause and effect. They look backwards for a connection between prior sin and present suffering. The Bible looks forward in hope and seeks explanations not so much in origins as in goals. [Scripture teaches us that] the purpose of suffering is seen, not in its cause, but in its result."[8]

The opening verse of chapter 1 gives us a clue as to the chief principle to be learned from a careful consideration of the book of Job. It is found in the words *the fear of the Lord.* Job lived in reverential awe of God. He was content to live under God's sovereign control of his life, and he turned away from evil. As a result he was both happy and successful. And when he was baffled by extreme and unexpected trials, he still held fast to his integrity. What he wanted most was an explanation of the cause of his suffering. Instead of being given an answer to his oft repeated request, the Lord, in His sovereign kindness, taught him new lessons and then blessed him above and beyond all that he could have asked for.

An anonymous author once wrote:

I have been through the valley of weeping,
  The valley of sorrow and pain;
But the "God of all comfort" was with me,
  At hand to uphold and sustain.

---

8. F. I. Anderson, *Job: An Introduction and Commentary* (Downers Grove, IL: InterVarsity Press, 1976), 68.

When He leads through some valley of trouble,
His omnipotent hand we trace;
For the trials and sorrows He send us,
Are part of His lessons in grace.

As we travel through life's shadowed valley,
Fresh springs of His love ever rise;
And we learn that our sorrows and losses,
Are blessings just sent in disguise.

CHAPTER TWO

THE REWARD OF THE RIGHTEOUS

The Patriarch's Life in Uz (1:1-5)

There was a man in the land of Uz, whose name was Job; and that man was perfect[9] and upright,[10] and one who feared God, and turned away from evil.

And there were born unto him seven sons and three daughters. His substance also was seven thousand sheep, and three thousand camels, and five hundred yoke of oxen, and five hundred female donkeys,[11] and a very great household; so that this man was the greatest of all the men of the east.

And his sons went and held a feast in the house of each one upon his day; and they sent and called for their three sisters to eat and to drink with them.

And it was so, when the days of their feasting were completed, that Job sent and sanctified them, and rose up early in the morning, and offered burnt-offerings according to the number of them all: for Job

9. *Tam*, "blameless," not sinless; completely honest.
10. *Yashar*, "straight," implying that he was a man of integrity.
11. Female donkeys were highly prized in the ancient Near East for they could breed and produce offspring.

said, "It may be that my sons have sinned, and renounced God in their hearts." This Job did continually (1:1-5).

Job lived in a city that was the edge of civilization. It was surrounded by vast stretches of land, some of which was wild and desolate while other portions were arable. The wilderness area was a place frequented by brigands who roamed about freely. These wily nomads would descend with speed on a town or village, and plunder and pillage with no thought for the value of human life (cf. Judges 6:3, 33; 7:12; 8:10) or the rights of others (cf. Job 1:15, 17).

Job greatness was acknowledged by all who lived in the East. He was rich and influential. His many servants had diverse responsibilities, with some being charged with the care of his household, while others were required to look after his crops, and still others were responsible for his livestock.

In addition to being a respected chieftain, Job was known for his worship of *Yahweh*, the true God. How he came to know about the Lord is not told us, but he must be numbered among other non-Israelites who, like Enoch and Noah, Melchizedek and Balaam, had a clear knowledge of God.[12]

From this brief description we note that the biblical writer[13] treated Job's attitude and conduct both positively and negatively. He portrays him as a man of integrity who lived daily in reverential awe of God. In a word, he was devout, and morally upright, for he rejected what was wrong. He was not sinlessly perfect, but consistently honest in his dealings.

God rewarded Job by blessing all that he had. In the course of time He gave him seven sons and three daughters. Job had what may well be regarded as an ideal family, for in Scripture "seven" and "three" are symbolic of completeness, and are a clear token of God's favor.

God also blessed Job by enlarging his flocks and herds. This indicates that he was not a nomad, for such large droves could not be moved easily. We also observe that Job was an agriculturalist (Job 1:14); lived in a house (Job 1:10), and enjoyed a settled existence.

His children were privileged to enjoy the best of everything. His sons lived in their own homes (cf. 1:4, 13, 18-19), while their sisters probably stayed with their parents. Job's sons had been reared in such a way that they enjoyed mature autonomy. They undoubtedly had their own farms and livestock from which all their needs were supplied. And they appear to have had sufficient leisure time to entertain one another by holding regular feasts.

---

12. The writer sometimes uses the name *Yahweh* (that often appears in our Bibles as Jehovah or LORD) to describe the God whom Job worshiped. For the meaning and use of the name *YHWH*, see J. J. Davis' article, "The Patriarchs and their Knowledge of Jehovah," in the *Grace Journal* IV, 1 (Winter 1963), 29-43.
13. The writer probably was Moses. He had been trained in all the wisdom of Egypt.

But what are we to understand by the words "on his day" in 1:4? Several different ideas have been put forward, with the most plausible being the celebration of birthdays. These celebrations possibly lasted for a week.

It is interesting to note that no disapproval of their pleasant life is to be found in these verses, and we are not to conclude from this that they spent each and every day in idle frivolity. There is no hint of drunkenness or slothfulness in this verse. Instead, the fact that the brothers took it in turn to entertain all their siblings, highlights the happy environment in which they had been reared.

The biblical writer then shows how conscientious Job was, for after each of these parties he would summon each of his children and offer burnt sacrifices on their behalf. He feared that one or the other of them might have dishonored God by something they may have thought or said. Such sacrifices would have restored their standing before a just and holy God.

Offering these sacrifices was Job's continual practice. Evidence of this is borne out by the inclusion of "all his days."

The Patriarch's Adversary in Heaven (1:6–2:12)

The scene now shifts from the city of Uz to heaven.

Now it came to pass on the day when the sons of God came to present themselves before *Yahweh*, that Satan also came with them. And *Yahweh* said unto Satan, "Where

have you come from?" Then Satan answered *Yahwe*h, and said, "From going to and fro in the earth, and from walking up and down in it." And *Yahweh* said unto Satan, "Have thou considered my servant Job? for there is none like him in the earth, a perfect and an upright man, one who fears God, and turns away from evil.

Then Satan answered *Yahweh*, and said, "Does Job fear God for nought? Have You not made a hedge about him, and about his house, and about all that he has, on every side? You have blessed the work of his hands, and his substance is increased in the land. But put forth Your hand now, and touch all that he has, and he will curse You to Your face."

Then *Yahweh* said unto Satan, "Behold, all that he has is in thy power; only upon himself do not put forth your hand."

So Satan went forth from the presence of Yahweh (1:6-12).

Apparently there were set times when angelic beings[14] came before the Lord God to receive their new assignments. We are not told how often these assemblies were held, for

14. The phrase "sons of God" is used of angels in 38:7 and in Genesis 6:2. From this passage it is evident that Satan is a person, not just an evil influence. He engages in a conversation with the Lord, showing that he has intellect; he is antagonistic toward Job, revealing his emotions; and he determines to destroy Job, intimating that he has a will. His activities, however, are subject to the sovereign will of God. For a full discussion of Satan's personality and power, see D. G. Barnhouse's *The Invisible War* (Grand Rapids: Zondervan, 1965), 21-35.

that is not relevant to the story of Job. On this occasion Satan also came with them, and because he had no right to be there he alone was asked his business.

Humorists and cartoonists are prone to refer to him as "his Infernal Majesty," or "old Nick;" whereas Medieval artists invariably portrayed him in black with sneering lips, evil, blood-red eyes, and horns protruding from his head. But are these depictions of the devil accurate?

Ezekiel teaches us that Lucifer (later referred to in the New Testament as the "serpent," "the devil," "the accuser of the brethren," and "Satan") was the "the highest, most beautiful, most powerful, and wisest of all *created* beings.[15] Did he come to the assembly in all of his glory? Perhaps. We cannot be sure.

While someone has said that the devil's greatest achievement over the last two centuries has been to convince people that he does not exist, the information brought before us in this chapter gives the lie to such a belief. What took place on this occasion, therefore, is of great importance

15. The passage in Ezekiel 28:11-19 needs to be understood in light of Christ's words in Luke 10:18 (see also Isaiah 14:12-15). Ryrie's note in the *Ryrie Study Bible,* (p. 1306) is judicious and explains the tie between Satan and the "king of Tyre": "This section, with its superhuman references, apparently describes someone other than the human *king of Tyre*, namely, Satan. If so, Satan's unique privileges before his fall are described in [Ezekiel] verses 12-15 and the judgment on him in verses 16-19."

to us for it aids our understanding of the devil and his devices.

Of course the Lord knew where Satan had been and why he had come before Him. He, however, asked what he had been doing. To this question He received the surly and somewhat evasive reply, "From going to and fro on the earth, and from walking up and down on it" (1:7).

The Lord then asked Satan if he had considered His servant Job. His question opened the door for Satan to state the reason for his presence. His response can best be understood as a sneer, for he contemptuously asked, "Does Job fear God for nought?" His answer implied that Job had only served God because God had made him rich.

The first time we hear Satan speak is in the Garden of Eden. There he slandered God by insinuating that He had deliberately deceived Eve about the penalty she and Adam would incur if they ate from the tree in the middle of the garden (Genesis 3:1-5). What he said took the form of a question, "Has God indeed said ...?" Now, in Job 1:9, he again asked a question. This time he spoke directly to the Lord and slandered Job by asserting that Job had ulterior motives for worshiping God.[16] His accusation implied that Job only worshiped God because that was the way he could continue to prosper. Then he attempted to further defame Job by saying in effect, "Remove the hedge with which you have surrounded him, and his piety will vanish into thin air."

---

16. G. C. Morgan, *The Voice of the Devil* (London: Pickering & Inglis, n.d.), 19-21.

The Lord accepted Satan's challenge, and the stage was set to test Satan's malicious insinuation.

The Patriarch's Severe Test (1:13-19)

After Satan had left the presence of the Lord, we read:

And it happened on a day when his sons and his daughters were eating and drinking wine in their eldest brother's house, that there came a messenger unto Job, and said, "The oxen were plowing, and the asses feeding beside them; and the Sabeans fell upon them, and took them away: and they have killed your servants with the edge of the sword; and I only have escaped alone to tell you."

While he was still speaking, there came another [of Job's servants], and said, "The fire of God has fallen from heaven, and has burned up the sheep and the servants, and consumed them; and I only am escaped alone to tell you."

While he was still speaking, there came also another, and said, "The Chaldeans made three bands, and fell upon the camels, and have taken them away, yes, and killed your servants with the edge of the sword; and I only am escaped alone to tell you."

While he was yet speaking, there came still another, and said, "Your sons and your daughters were eating and drinking wine in their eldest brother's house; and, behold, there came a great wind from the wilderness, and struck the four corners of the house, and it fell upon the young men, and they are dead; and I only have escaped alone to tell you " (1:13-19).

When we remember that in the ancient Near East a man's wealth was estimated by the size of his flocks and herds, his servants who waited on him, and the number of his sons, we realize how intent Satan was on depriving Job of everything that could contribute to his wealth and happiness, and prestige within the community. Furthermore, in order to secure maximum impact, Satan arranged for the tragic news of 1:13-19 to come like hammer blows, one after another.

The Patriarch's Reaction to His Loss (1:20-22)

Let us imagine ourselves in Job's house, witnessing events as they take place. First, Job was told that the Sabeans, who were nomads that roamed about the Arabian Desert, took his 500 yoke of oxen and his 500 female donkeys, and killed his servants. While this servant was catching his breath, another one arrived with the sad news that the "fire from God" had fallen and burned up his 7,000 sheep and those who tended them. Of course, to accomplish this Satan had to orchestrate a massive lightening strike. Just then a third servant arrived to tell that Chaldean[17] marauders from southern Mesopotamia had robbed Job of his camels and mercilessly killed those who cared for them.

Each disaster had followed hard on the heels of the former one, but the worst was still to come. Satan had chosen the very day, when Job's oldest son was entertaining his brothers and sisters, to kill them. A powerful whirlwind

---

17. The Chaldeans of a later time were noted for being fierce predators (cf. Habakkuk 1:6-11).

swept across the desert and struck the house[18] in which they were holding their feast, and all ten died when the house collapsed on them.

Then Job arose, and tore his robe, and shaved his head, and fell down upon the ground, and worshiped; and he said, "Naked came I out of my mother's womb, and naked shall I return thither: *Yahweh* gave, and *Yahweh* has taken away; blessed be the name of *Yahweh*."

In all this Job did not sin, nor did he charge God foolishly.

The rending of the robe or mantle, was the conventional mark of deep grief (cf. Genesis 37:34). Those living in the East wear a tunic or shirt, and loose pantaloons, and over these a flowing mantle. Shaving the head was also widely used as a mark of deep grief (cf. Jeremiah 41:5; Micah 1:16).

Satan, of course, hoped that Job would be so overcome with grief at the loss of his wealth and his family that he would curse God for dealing with him in this way. Job knew nothing of what had taken place in heaven, and so was at a loss to know why these misfortunes had overtaken him, but in spite of this he did not blame God for what had happened.

---

18. The house was probably situated in the farmlands, since it was the only house destroyed. Satan's action in demolishing only this house would have made it easy for Job's associates in Uz to conclude that either Job or his son(s) had sinned in some way and that is why he (they) had been singled out for punishment.

As Dr. Francis Anderson has pointed out, Job's attitude was clear. Satan's calloused criticism of God and Job's predicted reaction to misfortune proved false. Job did not worship God for the side-effects of prosperity. He knew that all things belong to God, absolutely, to be given as a gift, not claimed as a right. Job knew that the Lord is the sovereign owner of all, and he rejoiced in this wonderful fact.[19]

SOMETHING TO THINK ABOUT

Albert Barnes, in his *Notes* admonishes us to consider the example of Job. He points out that true godliness is able to endure the loss of property and friends without murmuring. Evidence of God's blessing is not based on such things as wealth or power or influence. It is founded deep in the soul, and mere external changes cannot destroy it. From Job's example we see the power of his Godward relationship in sustaining him in a time of severe trial.

What then is the "reward of the righteous"? Asaph admitted, "The nearness of my God is my good" (Psalm 73:28; see also Isaiah 58:2), and Job spoke from his heart when he said, "Though He slay me, yet will I trust Him" (13:15).

---

19. Anderson, *Job*, 88-89.

Send forth, O God, Your light and truth,
And let them lead me still,
Undaunted in the paths of right,
Up to Your holy hill ....
O why, my soul, are you cast down?
Within me, why distressed? ...
To Him my never failing Friend, I bow ...
To Him shall thanks and praise ascend,
My Savior and my God.
–John Quincy Adams.

CHAPTER THREE

A SHELTER IN THE TIME OF STORM[20]

During World War II the five sons of Thomas and Alleta Sullivan left their home in Waterloo, Iowa, to join the navy. They had only one stipulation, namely that they serve together on the same ship. In due time they embarked on the *U.S.S. Juneau* and sailed for the South Pacific. Six months into their deployment the ship was sunk and the five Sullivan brothers were lost.

On January 11, 1943 news that their sons were "missing in action" was brought to the Sullivan home by Lieutenant Commander Truman Jones. The news was devastating. To lose one son would have been bad enough, but to lose all five at once was more than those living at 98 Adams Street could comprehend. The big house seemed suddenly empty.

How did the Sullivans respond? They pulled together. The women supported one another as they coped with their fears and feelings of depression; and Thomas went back to work because he knew that this was what his sons would have expected him to do. Life would never be the same, but they knew they could survive by lovingly supporting one another.

---

20. Taken from Psalm 32:7.

Their experience was similar to (though not exactly the same) as Job's. He lost all his children and all his wealth on one day. But Satan's malevolent scheme did not end there.

Job's Opponents (2:1-10)

It came to pass on another occasion when the sons of God came to present themselves before *Yahweh*, that Satan[21] came also among them to present himself before *Yahweh*. And *Yahweh* said unto Satan, "From whence do you come?" And Satan answered *Yahweh*, and said, "From going to and fro on the earth, and from walking up and down on it."

And *Yahweh* said to Satan, "Have you considered My servant Job, for there is none like him on the earth, a perfect and an upright man, one who fears God, and turns away from evil: and he still holds fast his integrity, although you moved Me against him, to destroy him without cause."

And Satan answered *Yahweh*, and said, "Skin for skin! Yes, all that a man has will he give for his life. But put forth Your hand now, and touch his bone and his flesh, and he will renounce You to Your face."

So *Yahweh* said to Satan, "Behold, he is in your hand; only spare his life."

Then Satan went out from the presence of *Yahweh* and smote Job with sore boils from the sole of his

---

21. The definite article appears before *satan*, and has caused confusion for translators. It may be the biblical historians way of identifying Satan as "*the* Adversary" or "*the* Accuser" or "*the* Slander."

foot unto his crown. And Job took a potsherd to scrape himself while and he sat among the ashes.

Then his wife said to him, "Do you still hold fast your integrity? Curse God, and die." But he said unto her, "You speak like one of the foolish women. What? Shall we indeed receive good at the hand of God, and shall we not receive adversity?"

In all this Job did not sin with his lips.

Satan's Opposition (2:1-8). Once more the sacred writer conducts us to the courts of heaven. Imagine that you are an onlooker. The atmosphere is tense. The angels, all dressed in glistening white, are there. They know what transpired the last time Lucifer (Satan)[22] appeared among them. But why has he come a second time?

The Lord speaks directly to Satan about His servant Job. He reminds him that He has allowed him to unjustly afflict Job, yet Job still holds fast his integrity and remains loyal to Him. Satan is acutely aware of the fact that his efforts to prove that Job has only served God for the benefits he received, has failed. Now, however, he has a new strat-

---

22. When Satan rebelled against God (Isaiah 14:14) he was expelled from heaven, though he still has access there. He was thrown down to the earth (Luke 10:18) and now has liberty to roam about on the earth. According to Revelation 12:12 he will continue to exercise this freedom until he is bound during the Millennium and confined to the abyss for one thousand years. At the end of the Millennium he will be released for a short time (Revelation 20:2) before being thrown into the lake of fire for all eternity (Matthew 25:41).

egy. His cynical retort, "Skin for skin ...," reveals that he is totally devoid of compassion: In his new slanderous accusation he implies that a man will give all of his possessions in exchange for his life.

Something of the true nature of the devil is to be found in his retort, for it is disrespectful, and he does not cringe from disputing with the Lord of glory. Previously he had accused God of placing a hedge of protection around Job, now he asserts that if God attacked Job's body he would turn on God and curse Him to His face.[23]

The essence of Satan's accusation is based on the belief that Job was not hurt by the calamities that resulted in the loss of his family and wealth because all he cared for was himself. He snidely accuses the Lord of placing a hedge around Job and claims that if He now caused him physical harm, he would turn in retaliation on God–and curse Him to His face.[24]

---

23. Cf. J. E. Hartley, *The Book of Job*, New International Commentary on the Old Testament (Grand Rapids: Eerdmans, 1988), 78-79; N. C. Habel, *The Book of Job*, Old Testament Library (Philadelphia: Westminster, 1985), 94-95; and D. J. A. Clines, *Job* (3 vols.), Word Biblical Commentary (Dallas, TX: Word, 1989), I:40-41.
24. Though in the first round it was natural forces and lawless tribesmen who, at Satan's instigation, brought such pain and anguish on Job, it was God Himself who sovereignly permitted the devil to assail him. The reason why will only become apparent at the end of the book.

When the Lord gave Satan permission to afflict Job's body, he lost no time in setting about his malicious plan to afflict as much pain and suffering on Job as he could. This he did by causing very painful "boils" to erupt all over his body.

There has been a great deal of speculation about Job's affliction. Does *sehin* refer to "boils" or to some other extremely painful, disfiguring disease? Many modern scholars are of the belief that *sehin* refers to either leprosy (cf. Leviticus 13) or elephantiasis. The nature of Job's illness can only be understood if we consider all that the Bible tells us. Dr. Charles Ryrie has a note in his study Bible in which he draws together all of the ailments which made Job's disease both repulsive and painful: "The skin covering his entire body was affected (2:7), he itched intensely (v. 8), and he was in acute pain (v. 13). His flesh attracted worms and became crusty and hard (7:5). It oozed serum and turned dark in color (7:5; 30:30). Job also experienced fever and aching bones (30:17, 30). He may have had elephantiasis or a leukemia of the skin."[25]

Reduced to unending suffering, Job sat on the ash heap away from human company, and scraped himself with a broken piece of pottery because of the incessant itch (and perhaps to scrape away the pus oozing out of cracks in his skin).

---

25. *Ryrie Study Bible* (1995), 781. See also Anderson, *Job*, 91-92.

Job's Wife's Suggestion (2:9-10). It is at this point that Satan moves Job's wife to deride Job for his piety: "**Do you still hold fast your integrity? renounce God, and die.**" In saying this she urged her husband to do exactly what the devil had said he would do. But Job responded to her by saying, "**You speak like one of the foolish women. 'What? shall we receive good at the hand of God, and shall we not receive evil?' In all this did not Job sin with his lips.**"

Commentators are divided in their interpretation of Job's wife's actions. Some try to exonerate her, while others condemn her.

Those who attribute the best of motives to Job's wife point to the fact that she had suffered the loss of her children, and certainly this must have pained her greatly. She also saw her husband suffer from a cruel disease that caused him to leave the house and sit on the dung heap like a leper. They believe that in all of these situations her kind heart was torn, leaving her distracted and unable to cope with the complexities of her life.

In the "Testament of Job"[26] the writers give Job's wife the name, Sitis, and portrays her as a female slave, reduced to poverty and having to do all sorts of menial work in order to earn enough bread (which she dutifully shared with her husband) to sustain life. There are many incongruities in this story, but this ancient writing does place her in a good light.

---

26. Charlesworth, J. H., ed., *The Old Testament Pseudepigrapha*, 2 vols. (Garden City, NY: Doubleday, 1983), I:839-68.

Those who do not treat Job's wife favorably include many of the great men of Christendom: Augustine referred to Job's wife as Satan's diabolic assistant, Chrysostum believed her to be the devil's "best scourge," and John Calvin treated her as the "arm" of Satan.

Job's crops had not been affected when Satan caused him to lose all his wealth, and so his wife would have had food to live on. And we do not doubt that she shared the produce of the field with her husband.

But what caused her to criticize him for retaining his integrity? If we put her words in the mouths of some women today we might hear them say, "What good is your religion? Look at yourself. Your skin has become hard like an elephants, and your friends have deserted you. Why continue to suffer in this way? Your religion hasn't made you immune from suffering! Curse God and die." Is such an explanation too harsh? Let it be remembered that a wife's greatest gift to her husband is encouragement!

What modern interpreters must do is weigh carefully the fact that Job's wife's words "*curse*" and "*die*" are imperatives. Did she utter these words because she could no longer bear to see him suffer, or are they evidence of the fact that she had no enduring faith of her own and looked upon death as the only way to resolve the heartache they both felt?

Instead of helping Job, his wife's words caused him more pain and placed on him an even greater burden. His rebuke of her is revealing. He indites her for speaking like one of the common women. His use of the word *nabal*, “fool”, is revealing. But he did not leave matters on this negative note. He went on to admonish her with some practical counsel: “Shall we indeed accept good from God and not accept adversity” (2:10, NASB). No, adversity in whatever form it comes is designed by God for our ultimate good.

In all this Job did not sin. “Not only *good* but also *adversity* come from God to test and discipline us, and not necessarily as a punishment for sin.”[27]

The Visit of Job's Friends (2:11-13)

Job is described as the “greatest man of all the men in the east” (1:3*b*), and as such he must have had many influential friends. In the course of time word of his misfortunes spread and three of them, each a notable leader of his tribe, decided to meet and come to Uz to offer their condolences.

> **Now when Job's three friends heard of all this adversity that had come upon him, they came every one from his own place: Eliphaz the Temanite, and Bildad the Shuhite, and Zophar the Naamathite; and they made an appointment together to come to bemoan him and to comfort him. And when they lifted up their eyes afar off, and knew him not, they raised their voices, and wept; and they tore every one his robe, and threw dust over their heads toward heaven. So they sat down with him upon the ground seven days and seven nights, and no one spoke a word to him: for they saw that his grief was very great.**

---

27. Ryrie, *Study Bible*, 781.

The areas from which these men came were dealt with in Chapter One. We now find it profitable to consider their demeanor as they drew near to Job's home. When they saw him they could scarcely believe their eyes. His appearance was awfully changed, and they hardly recognized him as their old friend. What they had heard of his suffering paled into insignificance as they looked at him. It is no wonder that they "raised their voices and wept." Their expression of grief was accompanied by each one rending his mantle. Then they knelt down in typical Oriental fashion and threw dust upwards into the air so that it fell upon their heads and shoulders.

So great was their grief, and so completely did they enter into Job's suffering, that they sat in silence on the ground for seven days and nights with no one speaking a word to him. This does not mean that Job and his friends did not move at all during this time, for obviously they would have slept, eaten food, and relieved the needs of nature. What it does mean is that they spent as much time with him as possible, without intruding into his grief.

And no one spoke a word. Eastern courtesy requires a person to remain silent in the presence of one who is suffering great grief, and to wait for them to break the silence.

SOMETHING TO THINK ABOUT

The great Scottish preacher and poet, Dr. Horatius Bonar (1808-1889), wrote:

I dare not choose my lot,
  I would not if I might,
Choose Thou for me, my God,
  So shall I walk aright....

Take Thou my cup, and it
  With joy or sorrow fill,
As best to Thee may seem,
  Choose Thou for me my good and ill....

Choose Thou for me my friends,
  My sickness or my health,
Choose Thou my cares for me,
  My poverty or wealth....

Not mine–not mine the choice,
  In things both great and small,
Be Thou my Guide, my Strength,
  My wisdom and my all.

CHAPTER FOUR

THE PATRIARCH'S LAMENT

Early in my ministry a young man named Jeremy visited me. It was clear from the moment he entered my office that he was very upset. We exchanged greetings, and I noticed that his voice was raised. It was plain that he was angry. I motioned for him to sit down on one of the two comfortable chairs in my office, and I chose the other.

"What may I do for you, Jeremy," I asked.

"I don't know. Probably not much!" was his reply.

I waited for him to explain the reason for his visit. He took a deep breath, and then continued,

> "I'm a Christian. I read my Bible every day, and I try to follow its teaching. I've also tried to follow the teaching of the Book of Proverbs. You see, my parents have been poor all their lives, and I want to be successful so that I can provide something better for my family when I have one.
>
> Two years ago I married my highschool sweetheart, and we've established a happy home. But now my wife has told me we are expecting a baby, and try as I might I cannot figure out any way whereby I can support a family. I've prayed, but I haven't received an answer. We've budgeted, but we always come up short. What I see looming before me is the same kind of near-poverty

lifestyle as my parents. Where is God in all of this? I've followed the teaching of His Word, but somehow I feel as if He's let me down!"

Jeremy and I talked for a long time as we discussed his options. He was obviously a man of integrity, but he was also frustrated and fearful and equated wealth with happiness. Before he left my office we prayed together and I promised to see him again the next week; but he didn't keep the appointment.

Meeting with Jeremy reminded me of a poem by an anonymous author that I had read years earlier:

Happiness is like a crystal,
Fair and exquisite and clear,
Broken in a million pieces,
Shattered, scattered far and near.
Now and then along life's pathway.
Lo! Some shining fragments fall;
But there are so many pieces,
No one ever finds them all.

We all desire peace and a measure of prosperity, and we have been taught that if we order our lives correctly these blessings will be ours. But what are we to do when the circumstances of our lives contradict the belief system upon which we base our hopes?

Outline

The opening two chapters of the book of Job were written in prose, but with chapter three the writer begins a long section of poetry (3:1–42:6). Then 42:7-17 is again written in prose.

As we read chapter 3 we note that Job finally broke his long silence. He had endured great physical, mental and emotional pain, and in spite of his suffering he continued to believe that God always blesses the righteous and afflicts the wicked. Judging from his own experience, however, he was forced to conclude that God had not acted in accordance with his (i.e., Job's) beliefs. Still he clung to his integrity, though at times he gave way to hostility on account of his frustration and disappointed hopes. In spite of these outbursts he continually returned to his belief in God, even though he could not explain why such calamities had befallen him.

The Patriarch's Suffering (3:1-26)

Job Curses the Day of His Birth (3:1-10). After sitting on the garbage dump with his friends for an entire week, Job's long silence was finally broken.

> **Job opened his mouth, and cursed his day of his birth. And he said: "Let the day perish wherein I was born, and the night which said, 'There is a man-child conceived.' Let that day be darkness; let not God from above seek for it, neither let the light shine upon it. Let darkness and the shadow of death**

claim it for their own; let a cloud dwell upon it; let all that makes black the day terrify it. As for that night, let thick darkness seize upon it: let it not rejoice among the days of the year; let it not come into the number of the months. Behold, let that night be barren; let no joyful voice be heard. Let those curse it who curse the day, who are prepared to rouse Leviathan. Let the stars of its twilight be darkened; let it wait for light but have none, and let it not see the breaking dawn;[28] because it did not shut the opening of my mother's womb, or hide trouble from my eyes" (3:1-10).

At first we are shocked by the tone of Job's words, for we have come to expect only saintly statements from his lips (cf. 1:20-22). But when we consider the duration and severity of his suffering we are more inclined to ask ourselves how he endured so much for so long.[29]

Dr. Merrill F. Unger provides some interesting insights into the patriarch's condition. He asks rhetorically, "What caused the drastic change in Job from godly, patient submission to his sufferings to impatient imprecations? Although

28. Lit., "the eyelids of the morning" (cf. Sophocles, *Antigone*, 1:103).
29. It had taken several weeks for news of Job's misfortunes to reach his friends and for them to arrange to meet and journey together to Job's home with the expressed purpose of "comforting" him, and all this time he had patiently endured the intense pain and discomfort of the disease Satan had inflicted on him.

many natural causes for this alteration may be surmised, such as the erosion of his spiritual resistance by the unrelenting bout with his physical affliction, and the sight of his distinguished companions, which recalled too vividly his own splendid past now vanished, even though the underlying cause was satanic inroad though his would-be comforters."[30]

Some light is shed on the intensity of Job's suffering when we consider that the word used to describe the "boils" that covered his body (2:7) is the same word used to describe one of the plagues of Egypt (Exodus 9:8-12). The suffering of the magicians was not as acute as Job's, for each ones boils did not cover their entire body, and yet they were unable to stand in the presence of Pharaoh because of the pain. Seen in this context we marvel that Job endured such intense suffering with equanimity.[31]

Job Questions the Purpose of His Life (3:11-19). Job had lamented the fact that he had not been stillborn. Because this had not happened, he now stated that he wished he had died soon after being born.

---

30. Unger, *Commentary on the Old Testament*, 683. See also J. Kitto, *Daily Bible Illustrations*, 2 vols. (Grand Rapids: Kregel, 1981), II:55-56, who has some astute observations on these verses.
31. Ancient pagan sorcerers claimed to be able to curse a particular day and thereby make it unlucky (3:8). Job says in effect, "If those who practice witchcraft claim to have the power to rouse Leviathan (a mythological sea monster), then surely they could have prevented his conception and/or birth.

> **Why did I not die from the womb? Why did I not give up my spirit when my mother bore me? Why did the knees receive me? Or why the breast, that I should suck? For now should I have lain down and been quiet; I should have slept;** [if I had died soon after birth] **I would have been at rest with kings and counselors of the earth, who built up waste places for themselves; or with princes that had gold, who filled their houses with silver: or as a hidden untimely birth I had not been, as infants that never saw light. There the wicked cease from troubling; and there the weary are at rest. There the prisoners are at ease together; they hear not the voice of the taskmaster. The small and the great are there: and the servant is free from his master (3:11-19).**

The venerable patriarch, having expressed his desire that the day of his birth might be blotted out so that he might never have been born, next passes on to the wish that inasmuch as he had been born, he might either have died immediately upon his birth (3:11-15)[32] or else have been born dead (3:16-19). Either of these possibilities would have spared him his present misery. In either case he would have been at rest (even though to the Hebrews of a later period the grave was a shadowy, cheerless existence).

As we meditate on verses 11-19 we come to understand the depth of Job's agony for had he died he would have been

---

32. "Why did the knees receive me ... or why the breasts that I should suck" refer to the father's formal acceptance of the newborn child as his legitimate offspring, and the mother's nursing of her child in order to sustain his life.

free from the misery and pain that tormented him. And we can also reflect upon Satan's merciless cruelty that he would cause Job to be afflicted in such a way that he despaired of hope.

Job Longs in Vain for Death (3:20-26). Even now the patriarch wished that he might die, and likened his desire for it to those who diligently dig for hidden treasure. He felt as if he was hedged in, hemmed in by God with no comfort to ease his torment. His fears show that he had reached a place where he despaired even of good; and bitterest of all, he could not understand why God appeared to have forsaken him (cf. Matthew 26:24).

SOMETHING TO THINK ABOUT

Job was confused. His formula for life had seemingly failed him. He was at his wit's end. Antoinette Wilson knew what this was like and penned her famous poem "Wit's End Corner" to offer hope to those who are baffled by their suffering. Here, in part, is what she wrote:

Are you standing at "Wit's End Corner,"
  Christian with troubled brow?
Are you thinking of what is before you,
  And all you are bearing now?
Does the world seem against you,
  And you in the battle alone?
Remember–at "Wit's End Corner"
  Is just where God's power is shown.

Are you standing at "Wit's End Corner,"
Then you're just at the very spot
To learn the wondrous resources
Of Him who faileth not;
No doubt to a brighter pathway
Your footsteps will soon be moved

But Is the "God who is able" proved,[33]only at Wit's End Corner.

Job was at his wit's end. He could not understand why one misfortune after another descended upon him. He also did not know of Satan's involvement behind the scenes, and he [Job] did not know that he was being used by God as an example of unjust suffering.

33. The Internet contains hundreds of entries for "Antoinette Wilson." None of them led to the author of this poem. Further research indicates that this poem was included in a book entitled *Streams in the Desert* compiled in or about 1918 by Lettie (Mrs. Charles) Cowman. The frequent inclusion of this poem in different works, all prior to the 1920s, would indicate that it is now in public domain.

FIRST ROUND OF SPEECHES

CHAPTER FIVE

THE MORALIST'S REACTION

When Job's friends came to visit him they did so with every intention of comforting him in his distress. They sat on the refuse heap with him, and by their presence tried to empathize with him in his grief (cf. Ezekiel 3:15-16). After they had been with him for an entire week, Job broke the silence. He lamented the fact that he was suffering mentally and emotionally as well as spiritually and physically.

He was baffled because he had been neither complacent nor self-absorbed in his prosperity, and he had taken care not to forfeit God's favor. Yet what he feared most, namely, loss of God's approval, had happened to him and he could not explain why.

It is no wonder, therefore, that he was agitated and could not rest.

Such was Job's outpouring of grief that, when he had finished venting his anger, Eliphaz felt honor-bound to reply (4:1–5:27). He began courteously, but his reaction to Job's words soon took the form of a rebuke.[34] He acknowledged that in his time Job had been a support to and a teacher of others, but now that the vicissitudes of life had invaded the

34. See K. Fullerton, *Journal of Biblical Literature* (1929), 320-74.

serenity of his existence his attitude led him to conclude that he was incapable of handling adversity (4:1-6).

Eliphaz then attempted to explain why Job was suffering. In doing so he offered muted praise for Job's reverential awe of God, but implied that if Job was really a person of integrity he would readily recall that only the unrighteous suffer. Then to bolster his argument he appealed to Job's experience. He continued:

> **"According as I have seen, they that plow iniquity, and those who sow trouble, reap the same. By the breath of God they perish, and by the blast of his anger they are consumed (4:8-9)."**

This, of course, is a general truism, but obviously there are exceptions, however, Eliphaz did not deal with them, nor was he finished with his lame counsel. This may be deduced from the fact that he felt he need to give a second illustration. He pointed out that the impious man may be as mighty as a lion, but his home may be suddenly destroyed and his children forced to earn a living elsewhere.

Eliphaz then attempted to strengthen his argument by appealing to a "dream vision" he claims to have had. But this may have been little more than a cool breeze softly caressing his body at night, coupled with an over-active, superstitious imagination. The lameness of his supposed revelation does not add to our general understanding of the Lord or His ways. Note what he said to Job:

"Can a mortal man be more just than God? Can a man be pure before his Maker?[35] **Behold, He puts no trust in His servants; and He even charges His angels with folly: how much more them that dwell in houses of clay, whose foundation is in the dust, who are crushed before the moth!**[36] **Between morning and evening they are destroyed: Unobserved, they perish forever. Is not their tent-cord plucked up within them? They die, and that without wisdom"**[37] (4:17-21).

Job's friend must be commended for following what he believed to be the truth, but in the end it led him into error. He correctly exalted God's power and majesty, but erred in his belief by implying that if He cannot be bothered with angels, He certainly would not care about what happens to humans.[38]

Eliphaz' personal counsel was based almost entirely upon observation (5:2-27), and this minimized the value of his advice (5:8-16), reduced the value of his appeal (5:17-20), and made his personal promise of little worth (5:21-26).

35. It is difficult to determine how far the "dream oracle" goes. Does it end with 4:17, and do 4:18-21 contain Eliphaz' exposition?
36. The reference to the "moth" has provoked endless debate. The gist of the verse seems to be that human beings can be destroyed as easily as an insect.
37. Like a tent held up by only one cord.
38. Eliphaz's encounter with a spirit is suspicious for it does not contain any new evidence, which we would expect if the spirit were conveying information from God Himself.

He concluded his rebuke of Job with the assurance that he had personally verified all he had recommended (5:27).

Unfortunately modern-day would-be comforters like Eliphaz often do more harm than good through their counsel. Instead of encouraging a suffering person to reach out to the Lord, they imply that God does not hear prayer (cf. Psalm 66:18), and assert that those who suffer are obviously unrepentant (cf. Psalm 66:19).

It is easy to base one's belief on the notion that "**man is born unto trouble, as the sparks fly upward,**" but Eliphaz undermined the point he had been making by contradicting himself and stating that if he were in Job's position he would [39] "**commit his cause to Him who does great and unsearchable things.**"

It is difficult to determine what Eliphaz hoped to gain by this line of reasoning, except to elevate himself above Job now that Job had apparently become the object of God's disfavor. Then, having established his supposed superiority, he condescendingly said that if Job would follow his counsel, God would deliver him from all his troubles.

Eliphaz, however, discredited himself as a helper for in 5:21-26 he launched into a series of promises that did nothing to ease Job's pain or comfort him in his affliction. Then, in 5:27 he concluded by assuring Job that he had personally checked out what he advised, and invited Job to do the same

---

39. This type of egoism comes easily to a prosperous man who is not in the sufferer's place.

(as if Job's present condition would enable him to engage in such empirical investigation).

As a helper Eliphaz showed himself to be wanting in all the qualities of a wise friend.

SOMETHING TO THINK ABOUT

The noted evangelical scholar, Dr. William Henry Green, wisely observed that we can only properly appreciate the conduct of Job in his affliction if we take into account the fact that he became embroiled in his losses because he was unaware of Satan's malignant plan and lacked many of the firm supports of consolation that are now so readily available.[40] And given Eliphaz' personality, which was so antithetical to the support Job needed, it is no wonder Job felt used and abused.

Eliphaz' counsel failed to bring comfort to Job even though much of what he said was true. But it was not the whole truth. Underlying his entire argument was the one-dimensional assumption that all suffering is the punishment of sin. He failed to consider that some trials are designed by God to be corrective. And he failed to comfort Job because he did not deal with Job's felt need. All he succeeded in accomplishing was further burdening Job by adding to his affliction.

---

40. W. H. Green, *The Argument of the Book of Job Unfolded* (Minneapolis. MN: Klock & Klock, 1979), 77.

Eliphaz also failed to help Job because throughout he portrayed himself as a moralist rather than a sympathetic friend. What Job needed was empathic understanding, not arguments that brought him no help.

All of this reminds me of an incident that took place when I accepted a position on the staff of a Christian organization. After I had been introduced to the other employees, I sat down to enjoy some of the refreshments. I had no sooner done so when a young woman in her mid-twenties seated herself next to me and demanded, "When are they going to hire women counselors? I know my Bible as well as any man, and I believe that I could tell people what they should do."

I had taken a degree in marriage and family counseling, and even though my preparation had been mainly academic I realized that this young lady's approach would be much like Eliphaz', namely, directive and prescriptive rather than "paracletical"[41] and encouraging. Fortunately for me my work did not require me to have any professional interaction with her.

Some years later, another woman came to see me. It was plain to see that she was very distressed. She had just learned that she was pregnant and her husband had told her in no uncertain terms that they could not afford to have another child, and wanted her to have an abortion.

41. "Paracletical"--patterned after the Holy Spirit who is also spoken of in the New Testament as the Paraclete.

A friend of hers, a divorced mother, who counseled men and women in another church, advised her (and I quote exactly) to "Dump the 'bum' and keep the baby." We talked for a long time during which we discussed her options and what was best for her entire family. In the end she gave her husband time to adjust to the reality of having another mouth to feed, and kept both her husband and the baby.

The Christian community needs compassionate counselors–especially those who have an understanding of the Bible and the dynamics of human nature who have learned how to lead by asking appropriate open-ended questions, and know when to refer individuals to professional counselors.

As we reflect upon Eliphaz' counsel it should not surprise us to note that he failed in every point. He was patronizing and condescending, never identified Job's basic felt need, intruded his own philosophy of life into Job's suffering, and used his personal anecdotes to instruct Job.

The New Testament had not yet been written, but modern would-be helpers can learn a lot from the Apostle Paul's words in Galatians 6:1-4. He wrote:

> If someone is found to be at fault, you who are spiritual should restore him gently. But watch yourself, or you may be drawn into a similar situation. Carry each other's burdens, and in this way you will fulfill the law of Christ. If anyone [like Eliphaz] thinks he is something when he is nothing, he deceives himself. Each one should test his own actions. Then he can conduct him-

self appropriately without comparing himself to somebody else.

To be a people-helper one needs to understand the relationship between the mind, the emotions, and the will. The Holy Spirit has given each one of us certain gifts, and one of these is the gift of "helps." Let us humbly help one another so that the suffering believer can be lifted up and find hope in the midst of his/her suffering.

CHAPTER SIX

JOB'S REBUTTAL OF ELIPHAZ' MORAL ARGUMENT

How could Job possibly respond to Eliphaz' long-winded argument? He felt as if he had been kicked when he was down. Eliphaz had not helped Job bear his misery, but had intensified his frustration and distress. Now, however, in chapters 6 and 7 we have the patriarch's reply.

Job's Answer to His Friend (6:1-30).

Job's Renewal of His Former Defense (6:1-13). Eliphaz had reproved Job for his angry words, now Job responds by wishing that his earlier statement could be weighed against his calamity: "**Oh that my vexation were but weighed, And all my calamity laid in the balances! For now it would be heavier than the sand of the seas.**" He felt sure that such an act would provide adequate justification for his angry outburst (6:1-4).

Job's request that his remonstration be weighed against his suffering is not without merit. All his anger proved was that the Lord had caused him great pain. He then pointed out that even wild animals complain, and human beings do the same, so surely he was justified in voicing his grievance; for in his grief he could empathize with the wild donkey whose basic needs were not being met, or the domesticated ox who was suffering as a result of neglect (6:5-7).

Job then returned to a former, soon to be familiar, theme. "**What is my strength, that I should wait? And what is mine end, that I should be patient** [as I wait for death]**? Is my strength the strength of stones? Or is my flesh of bronze?**" His words expressed his frustration, and he believed that only death could release him from his suffering (6:8-12).

Job also believed that he would gladly face the pains involved in dying because he had confidence in his integrity. To him, death would be a way to ease his suffering, and because it was inevitable he asked, "Why should I wait for it? Why should it be postponed?" He knew that he did not have the strength of stones in a wadi or along the roadside, nor did he have the durability of bronze that would enable him to bear unending hardship.

The Failure of Job's Friends to Help Him (6:14-30). Job's experience at the hands of his friends is similar to many people in our churches; and there never seems to be lacking those within our assemblies who seem to have an answer to everyone else's problem(s), except their own. This point was borne out recently when my wife and I attended a party one evening. A person from our church came up to me and recommended that I pray for a woman who was having trouble in her marriage. I agreed to do so, however, I knew this man to be somewhat hypocritical and given to moral judgments without being able to cope with his own carefully concealed failings. In reality he was the one in need of prayer, for a few months later he separated from his wife and moved in with a married woman who was pregnant with his baby.

Job had defended his attitude toward his afflictions. But he was not finished. He evaluated the counsel of his supposed friends and found it wanting. Nor did he gloss over their unkind words. He likened them to torrents of water that rush down from the mountains only to sink into the desert sand so that travelers who expect to find a cool, refreshing river find only a barren gully. This is how he described his feelings:

> **"To him that is ready to faint kindness should be shown .... My brethren have dealt deceitfully as a brook, as the channel of brooks that pass away; which are black by reason of the ice, in which the snow hides itself: what time they wax warm, they vanish; when it is hot, they are consumed out of their place. The caravans that travel by the way of them turn aside; they go up into the waste, and perish. The caravans of Tema looked, the companies of Sheba waited for them. They were disappointed because they had hoped to find water, but found none (6:14-20).**

Job had not received from his friends the kind of sympathetic understanding he deserved, and as a result he felt keenly their rejection of him. And, even more painful than the attitude of his supposed friends was the heartache that accompanied his belief that he had been abandoned by the Almighty.

Job also likened his friends to being like mountain torrents, which in winter, offer an abundance of water which no one needs, but dry up in the heat of summer when people had an expectation of water. In his reply to them his use of desert merchants (6:19-20) further illustrates how he felt.

As the merchants from Tema and Sheba looked everywhere for water only to be disappointed, so Job had hoped for the consolation of his friends.

Job then reminded his friends that all he had expected of them was kindness and compassion. He had not looked for any favors or gifts (6:22-23). Then he said, "**If I have sinned, then tell me plainly what I have done wrong.**"

Verses 28-30 form a transition. Job had urged his friends to change their minds; and he pled with them, **"Teach me, and I will hold my peace; and cause me to understand wherein I have erred."** But when his pleading bore no fruit, he turned to rebuking them and asked, "**Your reproof, what does it reprove? ... Now therefore be pleased to look upon me; for surely I shall not lie to your face. Return, I pray you, let there be no injustice; yes, return again, my cause is righteous.**"

Job's Appeal to God (7:1-21)

Job's Description of His Condition (7:1-6). Job felt as if he had been plunged into the depths of hopeless despair. Though he did not know it the dark shadow of his "adversary" (the devil of 1:10-11 and 2:4-5) had been at work in Eliphaz, and all Job knew was that his expectation of convivial companionship with his friends had been dashed to pieces. He felt himself bereft of hope and enveloped in sadness from which he could not escape. He described his physical and emotional agony as similar to (1) the man who is compelled to endure long hours of forced labor; (2) a slave who toils in the hot sun and longs for some brief rest in a shady place, and (3) a hired laborer who waits eagerly for his wages.[42]

His feeling of helplessness was further exacerbated by his having to endure months of emptiness and weary nights when he tossed around on his bed waiting for the sun to peer over the eastern horizon. To further add to his misery, his sickness, instead of getting better, had gotten worse. His skin had become putrid, and exuded an ill-smelling puslike matter, and his loathsome sores had become infested with worms. And what was worse, his days passed without even a glimmer of hope. There was a monotonous sameness in his experience that was in itself depressing, and he concluded that his days would come to an end in frustration and despair.

Job's Soliloquy with God (7:7-21). Job's suffering was so intense that he had now given way to depression! He also lamented that his future could be measured as a handbreadth, and requested that he be allowed to go to Sheol (the place of the dead), and in the world of the unseen find peace.[43] At death he would vanish like a cloud, and would not return to the kind of life he had known before.

42. Unger, in his valuable *Old Testament Commentary*, 686-88, describes Job's suffering with true emotion.

43. *Sheol* in the Old Testament is the same as *hades* in the New Testament. *Sheol* is often used to describe physical death or the grave, and is the destiny of all humans. In Mesopotamian mythology it is referred to as "the land of no return." For a clear, definitive statement of the usage of the word *sheol*, see H. W. Holloman's *Kregel Dictionary of the Bible and Theology (Grand Rapids: Kregel, 2005)*, 499-500.

In this respect it is obvious that Job saw no hope of his life ever being different from his present pain-racked state. In doing so he gave vent to the intensity of his pain and the bitterness of his life. He asked rhetorically, "Am I the sea, or the sea-monster, that You set a guard over me?" It would appear as if Job was familiar with the pagan legend of the conflict between the sea-god Yamm and the weather-god Baal. If so, then he likened himself to Yamm who was defeated by Baal, and destined forever to be kept under certain restraints. Given these circumstances he would prefer death by strangulation rather than life.[44]

He continued his protest by complaining of God's constant surveillance of him. He likened himself to a prisoner who hoped sleep would ease his complaint, only to find his rest disturbed by those who kept guard at night. So continuous was this harassment that he did not have time "to swallow his saliva."[45]

He then asked rhetorically (7:17-18), **"What is man, that You should magnify him, and that You should set Your heart upon him, and that You should visit him every morning, and try him every moment?"**

Job's words, spoken in the midst of his despair, recall David's statement in Psalm 8, and give tacit proof that Job lived many years before David, and that David was cogni-

44. See *Ancient Near Eastern Texts*, 129-35, 137. It should be noted that Job did not contemplate suicide.
45. "Swallow my own spittle" is a Hebraic expression meaning "for a single moment."

zant of what the old patriarch had said. Years later Job's question, How can an infinite and holy God stoop to take note of what an insignificant, mortal man does?, was answered by David in Psalm 139.

Job lived in reverential awe of the Lord, and a part of this awe is a realization of God's watchfulness over us every moment of every day; and this is of great comfort to us who are unafraid in His presence.

There is much we can learn about suffering from Job's experience, and Aeschylus, the Greek poet, was most surely wrong when he wrote "Suffering when it climbs highest, lasts not long."[46] God used Job's suffering to teach us how to endure pain and hardship without giving way to the weakness of the flesh.

SOMETHING TO THINK ABOUT

An unknown author once wrote a poem which he or she entitled *Against a Thorn.*

Once I heard a song of sweetness
  As it cleft the morning air,
Sounding in its blest completeness,
  Like a tender, pleading prayer;
And I sought to find the singer,

46. Aeschylus, *Fragments*, 190.

Whence the wondrous song was borne;
And I found a bird sore wounded,
Pinioned by a cruel thorn.

I have seen a soul in sadness,
While its wings with pain were furl'd,
Giving hope, cheer and gladness
That should bless a weeping world;
And I knew that life of sweetness,
Was of pain and sorrow borne,
And a stricken soul was singing,
With its heart against a thorn.

You are told of one who loved you,
Of a Savior crucified,
You are told of nails that pinned Him,
And of a spear that pierced His side;
You are told of cruel scourging,
Of a Savior bearing scorn,
And He died for your salvation,
With His brow against a thorn.

–Anonymous.

CHAPTER SEVEN

THE TRADITIONALIST'S RESPONSE

We have all met with people who hold tenaciously to the traditions which they were taught by their parents or instructed in by their teachers, and Bildad the Shuhite was one of them. He was a traditionalist. Some traditions are valuable, but others inhibit the work of the Lord; and, as we read church history we find that the cause of Christ has often been crippled by those who held firmly to certain beliefs of the past.

The Doctrine of Retribution (8:1-7)

Bildad was a firm believer in divine retribution. As we pursue the continuing saga of Job and his three friends we find that Bildad lacked the polish of Eliphaz, and Zophar (who is yet to speak) was dogmatic to the detriment of the truth. Take note of Bildad's words. The inspired writer wrote:

> **Then Bildad the Shuhite said, "How long wilt thou speak these things? And how long shall the words of your mouth be like a mighty wind? Does God pervert justice? Or does the Almighty pervert righteousness? If your children have sinned against Him, He has delivered them into the hand of their transgression; if you would seek God diligently, and make your supplication to the Almighty; if thou were pure**

and upright, surely now He would awake [and come to your aid] (8:1-60).

As we look back it seems as if Bildad was outraged by Job's words to Eliphaz, and dismissed his defense as a "mighty wind–as tempestuous as it was empty." He also tried to vindicate God by asking rhetorically if God ever perverted justice. Furthermore he made no allowance for the fact that Job's defense of himself had been provoked by Eliphaz' misapplication of the truth.

Bildad's own words show him to be a man without pity. His entire denunciation of Job came from his creed. If he were alive today he would adroitly champion the cause of an extreme orthodoxy by quoting a Bible verse for every situation and condemning with other portions of Scripture all who dared to disagree with him. A person who has memorized portions of his/her Bible so as to be able to apply this knowledge to himself/herself as occasion requires is to be commended. In this regard Psalm 119:1ff. is an excellent case in point. But biblical orthodoxy needs to be tempered with love and compassion.

The wisdom of God's Word is of profound importance to everyone. To Bildad, however, his adherence to certain manmade tenets resulted in a lamentable myopia. Among these beliefs that formed the basis of his life-view was his assertion that all suffering is the result of sin. As he looked at Job sitting in mental and emotional anguish on the garbage dump, outside his home, and bereft of his children, he concluded that Job and his children had sinned.

I have encountered many people like Bildad–men and women–who are prone to use the Bible as a club. They have a proof-text for every situation and carefully prepared solutions for all the problems that human beings supposedly bring upon themselves.

Justification for this interpretation is to be found in Bildad's condemnation of Job's children (whom he did not know!) and his accusation that they had brought on themselves the judgment of God: **"If your children sinned against Him** (and he believed most assuredly that they had),[47] **He has delivered them into the hand of their transgression"** (8:4). This calloused statement completely disregarded Job's feelings, and all he did was add to Job's pain!

Then, in a statement that exhibited his pride and subtle feeling of superiority, he piously intoned, **"Then He would make your habitation prosperous. And though your beginning was small, yet your latter end will greatly increase"** (8:6b-7).

The Teaching of the Past (8:8-19)

Whatever may have been said in Bildad's favor (cf. 2:13), his harsh and unsympathetic condemnation of Job leaves us wondering if his creed left any room for empathy. His suggestion that Job take warning from the fate of his family only added insult to injury. And his recommenda-

---

47. In Bildad's theology to claim that Job's children had not sinned would make God an unjust Judge, for he believed that all suffering is the result of sin.

tion that Job diligently seek the Lord (*El*, God) and entreat the favor of the Almighty (*El Shaddai*)[48] was as empty as it was unnecessary.

As we have pointed out, Bildad was a traditionalist, and his own words support this conclusion. Note his recommendation to Job:

> **"Inquire now, I pray you, of the former age, and apply yourself to that which their fathers have searched out: (for we are but of yesterday, and know nothing, because our days upon earth are a shadow). Won't they teach you, and tell you, and utter words out of their heart?"** (8:8-10).

Building upon his supposed superiority (8:1-7), Bildad then assumed the role of a teacher (8:8-19). It was evidence of Bildad's haughtiness that he presumed to instruct Job.[49]

His statement that "**we are only of yesterday and know nothing**" was a further slap in Job's face, for what he implied was one's own experience, when compared with the wisdom

48. *El Shaddai* was the name God used when He revealed Himself to the patriarchs (cf. Genesis 17:1-8; 28:3-4; 43:14; 49:25), and underscored the fact that He is the all-sufficient One. The use of *El Shaddai* by Bildad, given his harsh words to Job, causes us to wonder if he had any real knowledge of the true God who was full of compassion.
49. Nearly all commentators are of the opinion that Eliphaz was the oldest of Job's friends, with Bildad being younger, and Zophar the youngest of all.

of past generations and a knowledge of history, is not alone the best teacher.

Bildad then reduced Job's problem to two simple analogies from nature. As the papyrus needs the wet mud of the river bank in order to grow, and the reeds along a stream need water or else they will quickly die, a person who forgets God will soon perish. Then, turning away from the analogy of nature, he once again slaps Job in the face by implying that his confidence in God is as flimsy as a spider's web. Note how he summarized his thoughts:

> **"So are the paths of all that forget God; and the hope of the godless man** (and that includes you, Job) **shall perish: whose confidence shall break asunder, and whose trust is a spider's web. He shall lean upon his house** (i.e., his faith), **but it shall not stand: he shall hold fast thereby, but it shall not endure"** (8:13-15)

Verse 19 is difficult to interpret. Taken in isolation it seems to promise hope, but when understood in light of Bildad's personality it seems to be a sarcastic statement meaning that the wicked can only look forward to "joy" in this life tempered, of course, by the certainty of calamity.

The Mistaken Guidance of a Dogmatic Traditionalist (8:20-22)

Dr. Merrill F. Unger has this to say about Bildad's closing comment. "With his mental processes enslaved in the shackles of a rigid syllogism [he] discovered that his prejudices were contradicted by the undeniable facts of experience. In the resulting spiritual tension, he found himself the subject of a mixture of self-assurance and uncertainty that half-heartedly comforted while it harshly condemned and held out a flicker of hope after it had already passed sentence."[50]

In Bildad's worldview he believed that Job's suffering had stamped the patriarch as a sinner. The only way Bildad could escape the dilemma he had created for himself was by resorting to his previous vague and undefined statement, "If you were ... upright" the Lord would forgive your sin and heal you. Then to show that he was not entirely without feeling, he expressed the faint hope that "**God would not cast away a perfect man, neither would he uphold evil-doers. He will still fill your mouth with laughter, and your lips with shouting. Those who hate you shall be clothed with shame; and the tent of the wicked will be no more**" (8:20-22)

Bildad had no faith in his provisional predictions. His consolatory statement was interrupted with what he really thought was applicable to Job.[51] His approach, however, made no allowance for different situations, and in this respect he was inflexible.

---

50. Unger, *Commentary on the Old Testament*, 690.
51. Ibid., 690.

SOMETHING TO THINK ABOUT

In this chapter Bildad has unjustly rebuked his suffering friend, and he had done so (as he supposed), to vindicate the ways of God. There is general truth in his affirmation that God deals differently with the upright and the evil, but his application of this general principle to Job is unsustainable.

In the Old Testament the Rechabites provide us with an illustration of the value of tradition. The Rechabites (1 Chronicles 2:55) were followers of Rechab, a descendant of the Kenites, and of the family of Jethro, Moses' father-in-law. They left Egypt with the Israelites and journeyed with them into Canaan, where they continued to hold on to their traditions. Because of the evils that were all about them, Rechab insisted that they not build houses (and so avoid the contamination of city life), and instead live in tents, never sow corn or cultivate vineyards or drink wine. These restrictions were designed to keep them from mingling with pagan idolaters.

So faithful were the Rechabites that they followed the traditions of the forefather and shunned city life for approximately 750 years. According to Jeremiah 35:1-19, they only came to live in Jerusalem when Nebuchadnezzar threatened to invade Judah. This shows that the tradition of Rechab had sufficient flexibility built into it so that when danger threatened they could make the necessary changes.

Traditions can be both helpful and harmful. In the New Testament *paradosis*, the word usually translated "tradition," has the root meaning of information "delivered" (i.e., as inspired, whether orally or in writing, by the apostles; cf. 1 Corinthians 15:3; see also 2 Thessalonians 2:15; 3:6,10). The only oral tradition designed by God to be obligatory on the church in all ages was soon committed to writing in the Apostolic Age. In only three passages does tradition have a good sense (1 Corinthians 11:2 margin; 2 Thessalonians 2:15; and 3:6); in ten it has the bad connotation implying man's uninspired tradition (see Matthew 15:2-3, 6; 8ff.; Mark 7:3, 5, 8-9, 13; Galatians 1:14; Colossians 2:8). Modern propagators of new theories or doctrines need to heed the words of the Lord Jesus who charged the Jews with "making the commandment of God of none effect through their tradition."

In an excellent summary of the biblical evidence, Dr. Henry Holloman wrote that the traditions of men result in vain religious beliefs, often learned by rote, without any sincerity of heart, practiced to be seen by people rather than God, causing people to transgress God's commands, and often hypocritical, replacing biblical doctrines with human ideas that have been handed down to successive generations, and cannot produce the kind of righteousness that is acceptable to God.[52]

Some Words from the Wise

Garnered from a Variety of Sources. Reader should use discernment, for all quotations are not of equal valve.

- By nature all men are sinners; by grace, they can be saved and become saints.
- There is hope for a sinner so long as he sincerely confesses and turns away from his sin.
- The greatest sin against one's fellow-man is selfishness; the greatest sin against God is self-righteousness.
- The person who has light thoughts about sin does not have great thoughts about God.
- A human being cannot become too sinful for God to save him/her.
- There is much about life that we cannot explain. We are not called to explain everything, but to believe in Him who made and controls all things.
- When faith is real, though the flesh have its feelings and/or doubts, the spirit triumphs over them.

---

52. Holloman, *Kregel's Dictionary of Bible and Theology*, 544-45. As we continue to discuss different traditions with our spouse and/or friends, we can focus (1) on the Bible and the meaning of the word "inspiration;" (2) the existence and attributes of God; (3) the nature of the Lord Jesus as the God-man (including His virgin birth, atoning death, and bodily resurrection), and salvation; (4) the wisdom and works of the Holy Spirit; (5) the nature of Satan and his eventual overthrow and eternal punishment; (6) mankind, created in the image of God, and fallen due to sin; (7) the place and importance of the Church and its leaders; (8) and the events that make up the "last times." What teachings help us in our daily walk with the Lord, and which doctrines have proved to be an impediment to the growth of the Church?

- Faith's way is to cast all care upon the Lord, and then to anticipate good results from the worst conditions.
- First, last, and always it is by faith that we stand.
- The Christian's comfort increases or decreases in proportion to his faith in God.

CHAPTER EIGHT

JOB'S UNRESOLVED DILEMMA

Let us, as best we can, place ourselves in Job's position. He is weary. The unrelenting pain has sapped his strength and deprived him of the will to live. Worst of all, he cannot understand why the Lord appears to have forsaken him. He grieves over the loss of his children; his wife is no comfort to him, and as if these trials were not enough, he now has to put up with the scurrilous attacks of his friends.

His mental and physical faculties had left him sad and exhausted. In his innermost being he felt as if God had condemned him, but he did not know why. Sitting on the garbage dump he was conscious of his insignificance (9:1-10), aware of the impossibility of a human being to stand up to God (9:11-24). In his despair he accused God of being unfair (9:25-35). Then he expostulated with God for what he believed to be His callous treatment of him (10:1-7), and he reminded God of His gracious dealings with him in the past (which contradicted his present experience) (10:8-17). Job ended his soliloquy with a cry of despair (10:18-22).

Job's Confession of His Insignificance (9:1-10)

In his response to Bildad, Job said:

> **Of a truth I know that** [what you have said] **is so: but how can man be right with God? If one wished to dispute with Him, he could not answer him once in a thousand times. He is wise in heart, and mighty in strength: who**

has defied Him without harm? It is He who removes the mountains, they know not how, when He overturns them in his anger; who shakes the earth out of its place, and the pillars tremble; who commands the sun, and it does not arise, and sets a seal on the stars;[53] **who alone stretches out the heavens and treads upon the waves of the sea; who makes the Bear, Orion, and the Pleiades, and the chambers of the south; who does great things past finding out, Yes,** [even] **marvelous things without number. Look, He goes by me, and I do not see Him: He passes on also, but I do not perceive Him. Were He to seize** [me], **who could say to Him, 'What are You doing?** (9:2-12).

In his angry, critical remonstrance Bildad had correctly affirmed the justice of God, and with this Job was in agreement, but the question now was, How can weak, fallen man be right before Him? No matter how upright a man's cause might be, he is too weak and lacking in understanding to be able to defend himself successfully before an omnipotent and omniscient God. His power is such that He overturns mountains, commands the sun not to shine, subdues the sea, and places the constellations in their orbits.

Job's Admission of His Powerlessness (9:11-24)

Job, in his suffering, had envisioned God as remote and inaccessible.

---

53. This is a very difficult expression, and the Hebrew text sheds little light on it.

> **The helpers of Rahab stoop under him.**[54] **How then can I answer him,** [and] **choose out my words** [so as to reason] **with him? For though I were righteous, yet I could not answer; I would have to implore the mercy of my judge. If I had called and He had answered me, yet could I not believe that He was listening to my voice. For He bruises me with a tempest, and multiplies my wounds without cause. He will not allow me to get my breath, but fills me with bitterness. If** [we speak] **of strength, lo,** [He is] **mighty! And if it is a matter of justice, who con summon Him? Though I am righteous, mine own mouth shall condemn me** (9:13b-20a).

Job's words revealed his despair. He felt as if God had deserted him, and this left him feeling unloved and alone. The comfort of God's presence that he had known was now a memory. And worst of all he concluded that, for reasons he could not understand, God would not "turn back His anger" and have mercy on him. Though he believed himself to be upright, he knew he could not successfully plead his case before Him.

---

54. The gist of this verse implies that there are times when God does not restrain His anger until all earthly and cosmic powers are subdued before Him. Job cites a proof of His irresistible power in His victory over Rahab which in ancient mythology was a reference to the sea monster that lived in the depths of the sea (later a figurative name for Egypt, implying pride and arrogance). See Gibson, *The Book of Job*, 45, col. b.

All of this brought Job to a position of dejection and a feeling of hopelessness.

In this respect Job voiced the complaint of many since his time. Some tragedy strikes us (e.g., the loss of a family member who was taken before his/her time; the unjust firing of a person of integrity from a position of trust; the departure of one of our children from the godly principles in which he/she was reared; the loss of one's financial security; and any number of hurtful experiences), and God seems disinterested in us and far removed from the traumatic experience that is of great concern to us.

When we experience these setbacks we believe that God is no longer interested in us and is punishing us. But for what? We then see the wicked triumphing while He appears to ignore the pleading of those who turn to Him requesting His aid (9:22-24).

Job's Belief That God Had Been Unfair to Him (9:25-35)

Next Job succumbs to deep depression.

> **Now my days are swifter than a runner: they flee away, they see no good, they are passed away as the swift ships; as the eagle that swoops down on the prey. If I say, I will forget my complaint, I will put off my sad countenance, and be of good cheer; I am afraid of all my pains, I know that You will not hold me innocent. I shall be condemned; why then do I labor in vain? If I wash myself with snow water, and make my hands clean with lye, yet You will plunge me into the ditch, and mine own clothes would stick to me** (9:25-31).

Job gives four reasons for his complaint: (1) the brevity of life; (2) his sadness and fear, for he had unwittingly believed the devil's lie that God would not acquit him; (3) the futility of life and the emptiness of daily work; and (4) the dread of unforgiven sin which he likened to being thrown into a muddy pit with the result that his own clothes would stick to him.

In anguish of heart he cried out for an umpire, someone who would place his hand on God' shoulder and his own and bring them together. Of course, this need on the part of mortals was met in the person of the Lord Jesus Christ who is the only Mediator between God and human beings (1 Timothy 2:5). Lacking such a mediator Job was frightened as he contemplated God's omnipotence. He feared He would pronounce him guilty, only with more justification than his friends.

Job Turns to God in Prayer (10:1-22)

But Job still carried in his heart the weight of unanswered questions. And so he confessed to God exactly how he felt.

> **My soul is weary of my life; I will give free course to my complaint; I will speak in the bitterness of my soul. I will say to God, 'Do not condemn me; show me why You contend with me. Is it good for You to oppress, to reject the work of Thy hands, and to look favorably upon the counsel of the wicked? Do You have eyes of flesh? Or do You see as man sees? Are Your days as the days of a mortal, or Your years as man's days, that You inquire after my iniquity, and search after my sin, although You know that I**

am not wicked, and there is none who can deliver me out of Your hand?" (10:1-7).

Dr. Francis Andersen, the Australian theologian and author of an insightful commentary on the book of Job, reviewed Job's attitude and conduct. He pointed out that many of the thoughts and ideas Job had expressed earlier now recur. "Among their reiteration there emerges a new thought which gives Job fresh hope.... He cannot believe that God made him to end up in such a state. He must have something better in mind, even though at the present the only outcome he can imagine is the gloom of death."[55]

All this points to the fact that we lack a "theology of suffering." And yet, as we read through the gospels and the epistles we find numerous references to Christ's and Paul's experiences of pain and misfortune (cf. Mark 14:33; John 11:33; 12:27; 2 Corinthians 1:8-9; 4:8-11). Our tendency is to look upon any form of trial or misfortune as an indication of the fact that we are out of the will of God. But such is not necessarily the case (cf. Philippians 3:10).

In his prayer Job did not pray for healing. Instead, he focused on something which we tend to overlook, namely, God's remarkable care with which He prepared our human body and the seeming neglect He now shows for us in our sickness.[56] Then, as he continued his prayer he expresses confidence that God had a purpose that was good, and that it was inconceivable to him that God would "turn him to dust"

---

55. Anderson, *Job*, 151.

(10:9*b*), for this would be contrary to His *hesed* ("steadfast love").

There seems to be an abrupt transition marking the next section (10:14-17), but different translations handle it in different ways. In contrast to the quiet confidence (hope) expressed in 10:8-13 Job now appears to sink back into despair. It is true that he was exhausted, but how are we to explain his reference to God being indifferent to good and bad people? Job's reasoning is given in 10:15-17. Then in 10:18-22 two great themes intersect and seem to be in conflict, namely, God is powerful, and He is good. Job illustrates these two tenets (1) by referring to God's power in the wonders of creation, and (2) His beneficence in crafting each person's body and in giving him/her life.

Job cannot reconcile the tension created between these aspects of God's activity and so retires to an earlier position: he wished he had never been born, or had died before delivery, or had never ever been conceived. But since he had been born, he wished that he had died soon afterward.

At this point he either leaves off his prayer because of exhaustion, or is interrupted by Zophar (11:1-20), who to this point had remained silent.

56. The Hebrew text of 10:8-22 is difficult to understand. To gain maximum benefit from them readers should use a couple of accurate translations.

SOMETHING TO THINK ABOUT

When we are weighed down with care and everything in life seems out of kilter it is good for us to remember the words of the poem, "The Love of God," It is made up of two parts. Stanzas one and two were penned by a Lutheran pastor in 1917, while the concluding stanza was composed by Rabbi Mayer in Germany in 1996. They breathe encouragement to all who are downcast. Here are the now famous lines of stanzas 1 and 3.

The love of God is greater far than tongue
or pen can ever tell,
It goes beyond the highest star and reaches
to the lowest hell,
The guilty pair, bowed down with care,
God gave His Son to win:
His erring child He reconciled and pardoned
from his sin.

Could we with ink the ocean fill and were the skies of
parchment made,
Were ev'ry stalk on earth a quill and ev'ry man
a scribe by trade
To write the love of God above would drain
the ocean dry,
Nor could the scroll contain the whole tho stretched
from sky to sky.

The thoughts of this poem are worthy of continued reflection, for they breathe encouragement to all who are downcast.

CHAPTER NINE

THE DOGMATIST'S RESPONSE

Dogmatism is found among people of all ages and all strata of society. I recall with pleasure the time my wife and I took our sons, aged 3 and 5, for a walk along the bank of the River Thames. My sons were awed by the larger than life statues of men on horseback that were interspersed along the sidewalk. I pointed out Westminster Abbey and the Houses of Parliament (which attracted little interest on the part of my sons), and then we came to Big Ben.

My wife had taken our elder son on ahead of us, and so I turned to the youngest member of our family and asked, "Do you know the name of this clock?"

He looked at me quizzically and then replied with great confidence, "Clocks don't have names."

To this challenge to my wisdom I replied, "Yes, but this clock does have a name. It's called Big Ben."

"No it's not!" responded the youthful authority by my side.

I then made a tactical blunder. I said, "Yes, it is."

Pulling his hand out of mine and turning to face me, he said "No it's not!" His emphasis was unmistakable, and I gave up trying to convince him.

Dogmatism in a child may be corrected over time, but when it manifests itself in an adult– in the workplace, home, or church– it can cause rifts in one's relationship.[57]

Job, You're Nothing But a Windbag (11:1-6)

Job experienced this kind of dissonance in his relationship with Zophar who was probably the youngest and certainly the least intelligent of his "counselors." And Zophar was also the bluntest and most tactless of his friends. He was more harsh in his criticism of Job than his associates, and sided with them in their conclusion that Job was suffering because of his sins. Something of his calloused approach may be gleaned from the fact that he claimed God had only given Job a fraction of the punishment that he deserved. Then he pointed out that all Job needed to do was sincerely repent and everything would be made right.

As we weigh carefully Zophar's words we note that there is not an ounce of compassion in what he says, but only a censorious criticism of Job's defense of himself.

> **Should not the multitude of words be answered? And should a man full of talk be justified? Should your babbling make men hold their peace? And when you mock, shall no man rebuke you? For you say, "My doctrine is pure,' and 'I am clean in your** [or God's] **eyes." But oh that God would speak, and open His lips against you, and**

57. These issues have been discussed at length in Milton Rokeach's *The Open and Closed Mind* (New York: Basic, 1960).

> **show you the secrets of wisdom! For sound wisdom has two sides.**[58] **Know therefore that God punishes you less than your iniquity deserves** (11:2-6).

Zophar's cold disapproval shows how little he understood of Job's feelings. Unlike his friends who had other criteria to support their beliefs, Zophar had his own standard (i.e., himself). His wisdom was the determining factor in deciding what was right and what was wrong.

Job's outbursts were natural, given the duration and intensity of his pain, but to accuse him of being verbose was to do him an injustice. Zophar was sure Job was guilty, and if God would only speak He would show Job the limits of his own understanding. Little did Zophar understand his own arrogance. He provided no reason for his harsh judgment of Job and claimed that Job was getting off lightly with less punishment than his sin deserved. And in the end, to justify himself, he put words in Job's mouth.

Job, I Wish God Would Appear and Teach You True Wisdom (11:7-12)

Though Zophar's bitter criticism of Job is shorter than the lengthy statements by his friends, he was nonetheless convinced that he was right.

---

58. God's wisdom has two sides, the one that human beings see, and the other known only to God.

> **Can you by searching find out God? Can you find out the Almighty to perfection?** [Knowledge of Him] **is high as heaven; what can you do? Deeper than Sheol; what can you know? The measure thereof is longer than the earth, and broader than the sea..... For He knows false men** [like you, Job]: **He sees iniquity.... And an idiot** [like you] **will become wise when a wild donkey gives birth to a man** (11:7-12).

Zophar correctly concluded that God is all-knowing and all-sufficient with knowledge that no man can fathom. He is also all-powerful, and no one can restrain Him from doing whatever He pleases. But where, in all Zophar's abusive criticism, was there evidence of his compassion?

Having vented his bitter feelings toward Job, Zophar then stated (with an attitude of vaunted superiority) that God knows the truth about all human beings. He also implied that Job was wicked and God knew it–even though Job may have been unaware of his own wickedness. Then he closed this portion of his diatribe by asserting that Job would only gain intelligence when the foal of a donkey gave birth to a man.

Job, Learn From Me, Repent of Your Sins and God Will Bless You With Peace and Prosperity (11:13-20)

With verse 13 there is a transition. Zophar had apparently exhausted his meager knowledge and so turned to preaching.

> **If you set your heart aright, and stretch out your hands toward Him, if iniquity is in your hand, put it far away, and do not let unrighteousness be found in your tents; then surely you shall be able to lift up your face without defect** [guilt ?]; **and shall be steadfast, and shalt not fear. For** [then] **you would forget your misery, as waters that are passed away, and your life would be clearer than the noonday .... Then you would trust because there is hope, and look about you and rest securely. Also you would lie down, and none shall make you afraid; and many will seek your favor** (11:13-19).

Zophar's "sermon" was full of pious cliches, and even *if* his sentiments were well-meant, he lacked both the ethos and pathos that would have made what he said effective. And he still adhered to the belief that Job's problem was unconfessed sin.

In his bumbling way Zophar provided a beautiful resume of the tranquil life that awaited Job if he would only repent of his sin and reach out to the Lord. He even assured Job that people would flock to him because his prosperity would be proof of his closeness to God.

But Zophar's rehearsal of the blessings that would await Job if he but followed Zophar's counsel must have awakened painful memories in Job, for he described Job's life as it was before tragedy struck.

Zophar then concluded his sermonette by stating in verse 20 that **"the eyes of the wicked shall fail, and you** [Job] **will not escape. The hope** [of the wicked] **is to breathe their last.**"

* * * * *

Each of Job's friends has spoken, and one might assume that they had exhausted their arguments. Such, however, was not the case. Job had been unmoved by their often heated harangue, and he still sought after God, and longed for the former assurance of God's loving kindness toward him that he had once enjoyed.

The first round of counsel had run its course, and the second was soon to begin. Job's friends were more convinced than ever that he was covering up some sin, and they conceive it to be their duty to continue to call him to repentance, even though he continued to reject their well-intentioned ministry. He believed himself to be a man of integrity, but each protestation of his uprightness only caused his friends to upbraid him even more.

SOMETHING TO THINK ABOUT

Criticism should be constructive, not destructive (cf. Ephesians 4:2, 15; also John 8:45; Romans 12:10; 13:10; 2

Corinthians 5:14, 6:6), for dogmatic people are met with in all walks of life, and those that frequent Christian circles are by no means exempt.

At one time when I was enduring constant criticism a friend of mine gave me some good advice. He recommended that I imagine that I have a large closet in which there was an overcoat made of sponge. Then he recommended that whenever I became the object of a person's severe criticism, I remove from the closet this sponge overcoat and put it on. The sponge would then absorb the vitriolic venom of the person who wished me ill. When he (or she) had fully exhausted their anger I was recommended to take off the coat, wash it thoroughly, and replace it in the closet pending the next time I would need it.

I found this to be good counsel.

In what way(s) do you think Job was able to preserve his sense of worth when all comforts were removed?

Finally, let each of us be on our guard against those who negatively criticize us, for all they may be doing is obliquely commending themselves.

CHAPTER TEN

HOW TO ANSWER ONE'S CRITICS

With chapters 12, 13 and 14 we come to a transition. In spite of his pain and the weight of his unanswered questions, Job has listened with great patience to the harsh judgments and occasional ranting of his three friends.[59] Now with the final words from Zophar he chooses to respond to the vaunted knowledge and insensitive condemnation of his visitors. After this, they may decide to go their respective ways and leave him to his thoughts and solitary position on the garbage dump.

Job's vindication of himself was three-fold: (1) He denied that his wisdom was inferior to his friends and that his status was inferior to theirs; (2) He denied the premise of their accusations because it was based upon the false logic that the innocent do not suffer, that suffering is caused by sin, and that *in their eyes* his sufferings indicate that he must be a great sinner; and, (3) He denied the false premise that outward prosperity and good health are infallible indicators of either godliness or wickedness.

With the close of chapter 11 we come to the end of the first series of discussions. All the issues have been openly debated. Job, however, remains unmoved, and his friends remain obdurate. Job has not been swayed by their discussions, and is determined to be submissive to the irresistible

59. Job describes them as "miserable comforters" (16:2, KJV)

power of God. His friends, however, conclude that he is ignorant of the manner in which he has offended God. To their way of thinking God has exposed his secret sin, and Job's concealment of it is worse than whatever sin(s) brought on God's punishment.

In responding to the calumny of his critics Job holds tenaciously to his faith in the love and wisdom and sovereignty of God. Ella Wheeler Wilcox (1855-1919) put it this way:

I will not doubt, though all my prayers return
Unanswered from the still, white realm above;
I shall believe it is an all-wise Love
Which has refused those things for which I yearn;
And though at times I cannot keep from grieving,
Yet the pure ardor of my fixed believing
Undimmed shall burn.

I will not doubt , though sorrows fall like rain,
And troubles swarm like bees about a hive;
I shall believe the heights for which I strive
Are only reached by anguish and by pain;
And, though I groan and tremble with my crosses,
I yet shall see, through my severest losses,
The greater gain.

Job's Repudiation of His Friends Vaunted Knowledge (12:1-25)

Chapter 11:29-31 marks the end of the first round of speeches, but we are surprised by the difficulty posed in translating 12:2. Different translators have attempted everything from a very literal rendering of the text to attempts to make the verse intelligible to Westerners. As a result we are not surprised by their lack of agreement. David J. A. Clines' paraphrase is the best we have seen. "**Truly you are the last of the wise! With you wisdom will die! But I have intelligence as much as you; I am not inferior to you.**"[60] Dr. Cline captures the satire of Job's remark without emending the text as do so many other commentators whenever they are confronted with a difficulty.

In verses 1-6 Job denied three things: (1) He rebutted their insinuations that he was ignorant of the ways of God and in this respect inferior to the wisdom of his friends (cf. 11:12). In doing so he laid claim to the fact that his knowledge was based on what he had seen and heard personally, and not in tradition. (2) He denied their assertion that the innocent do not suffer, and (in the view of his friends) because suffering comes from sin, he must be a great sinner. This knowledge forms the basis for his desire to place his case before God. (3) He denied their bold claim that outward prosperity and health are necessarily indicators of a godly life. Job does not claim wisdom, but the knowledge that God uses wisdom to deprive human leaders of the kind of arrogance that comes from intellect and authority.

---

60. Clines, *Job*, I:275.

Then, in verses 7-12 Job rejects the false teaching of his friends. In doing so he points to nature and history as sources of divine revelation, and uses animals, birds and fish whose implanted instincts readily teach observant humans about the Lord.[61]

Next (in verses 13-25), Job showed the shallowness of his friends understanding of history and experience, for they had argued that the ways of God are always transparent, whereas each individual frequently faces personal trials and calamities (such as droughts or floods) that make the ways of God hard to discern. And, as the Almighty, He has a plan that He does not necessarily reveal to humans.

Job's Indictment of His Friends For Their Failure to Help Him (13:1-28)

Though Job was suffering intense physical and emotional pain, he had not suffered from any mental lapse. He resented the claim of his three "friends" who boasted of their superior knowledge, and this gave Job the opportunity to reiterate his belief that his knowledge was equal to theirs. **"Look, my eye has seen all that you see, my ear has heard and understood it. What you know, I also know: I am not inferior unto you" (13:1,2).**

But with this knowledge Job remained unsatisfied, and so he repeated his wish to speak directly to God: **"I would speak to the Almighty** [El Shaddai, the all-sufficient One]**, and I desire to reason with God.** [Though you pretend to speak for

61. Habel, *The Book of Job*, 223, 225-27.

God] **you are forgers of lies; you are all physicians of no value. Oh that you would altogether hold your peace, and it would be your wisdom!" (13:3-5).**

With these words Job emphatically rejected their bold, misdirected comments (cf. Proverbs 17:28). He asked for "equal time," stating that it was only fair that they listen to his argument. He resented the dishonor they had done to God, in claiming to speak for Him, whereas they had distorted what He had revealed.

Job then warned his friends of the inevitability of God's judgment. Could they deceive Him? And how would they fare when faced with His judgment? In verses 9-12 Job warns his friends of the danger they faced, for God would most assuredly punish them for their duplicity.

At this point one or all of his friends tried to interrupt him (13:13), but he said to them **"Hold your peace, let me alone, that I may speak."** Then he stated emphatically that he had found their defenses to be defenses of clay, and their memorable sayings only proverbs of ashes.

Job had before stated his confident standing before God, and now he reiterated his assurance that **"though He slay me, I will hope in Him.... This also shall be my salvation, for a godless man shall not come before Him"** (13:15,16).

Finally, Job turned to God in prayer. His entreaty consisted of seven questions and/or requests:

> How many are my iniquities and sins? (13:23*a*); Make known to me my transgressions (13:23*b*); Why have you

withdrawn Yourself from me? (13:24); How can I stand before You? (13:25); My afflictions are more than I can bear (13:26); Your surveillance of me makes me think that I am in prison (13:27); I am wasting away under Your heavy hand. I've become like a rotting thing, like a moth-eaten piece of clothing (13:27,28).

Does this kind of frustration and despair have a human ring to it? The celebrated lexicographer and poet, Dr. Samuel Johnson (1709-1784) wrote of the benefit we can all derive from prayer:

Father, in Thy mysterious presence kneeling,
Fain would our souls feel all Thy kindling love,
For we are weak, and need some deep revealing
Of trust and strength and calmness from above.

Job's Determination to Lay His Case Before God (14:1-22)

But Job was not finished. He wished to draw the attention of his "comforters" to human frailty and the inevitability of mortality. To do so he reminded them that "**Man, that is born of a woman, is of few days, and full of trouble. He comes forth like a flower, and is cut down: He flees also as a shadow, and does not remain**" (14:1,2) He is like a flower that appears for a short time and then withers away.

Then (in verse 13) he asked, "**Who can bring a clean thing out of an unclean?**" And he answered his own question: "**No one.**" Of course Job lived many years before the

Lord Jesus died to make atonement for the sins of all who turn to Him in faith requesting His forgiveness and salvation.

But what of life beyond the grave? Here Job provides an analogy from nature. "**For there is hope of a tree, if it is cut down, that it will sprout again ... and though the root grows old in the earth, and the stump dies in the ground; yet through the scent of water it will bud, and put forth shoots like a plant. But when humans die they lie prostrate ...**" (14:7-10) and give no evidence of life after death.

Job, of course, knew nothing of the resurrection of Christ, and consequently all he could do was give voice to his personal belief in life beyond the grave. Once again he asked a question and then answered it: "**If a man dies, shall he live again? All the days of my pilgrimage I will wait, until my change comes. You will call, and I will answer You...**" (14:14,15) Then he added a thought that was probably totally new in his day, that mountains may crumble and streams dry up and torrents sweep away the soil, yet God remains the same, and He forever changes the appearance of those who die trusting in Him.

SOMETHING TO THINK ABOUT

For many years the late Oswald J. Smith (b. 1889) pastored the People's Church, Toronto. He was a man of many talents: author, missionary statesman, poet, and preacher par excellence.

On one occasion he wrote:

O Thou who seest all my grief,
The anguish of my heart,
The disappointments, trials and cares,
That make the tear drops start;
O Thou whose love has never failed
Though dark the night and long,
To Thee I turn my weary eyes
And hope springs forth in song.
O Thou who knowest all my thoughts,
The hunger of my soul,
The blighted hopes of bygone years,
The dreams of life's lost goal;
The aching void, the loneliness,
And all the thornclad way,
To Thee I turn with faith undimmed
And 'mid the darkness pray.

O Thou who givest grace and strength
For every trying hour,
Who understandeth when I fall
Before the tempter's power
O Thou who dwellest in my heart,
Whose will is my delight,
To Thee I turn, Thy face I see
And all again is bright.[62]

62. Marshall, Morgan and Scott, Oswald Smith's London publisher, copyrighted all his poems in 1962. MM&S have since gone out of business and I have been unable to find a more recent copyright holder. I presume, therefore, that "A Prayer in the Night" is now in public domain. If not, I shall be happy to give full credit in a later edition of this book.

SECOND ROUND OF SPEECHES

CHAPTER ELEVEN

WHEN ANGER TAKES OVER

Before the Hawaiian island of Maui experienced an influx of new residents there was a two-lane road that circled its northern and southern sections. Traveling along this road visitors would come eventually to Nakalele Point where black lava from an early volcanic eruption had run into the sea. The powerful waves that pound this section of the island gradually opened up two large blowholes. These blowholes fascinate visitors, for each time a wave breaks upon the black lava a mixture of sea water and spray is flung through these holes into the air.

Partly because of the roar that accompanies the thrusting of seawater and spray through these blowholes, people have begun referring to individuals who frequently give way to their anger as "blowholes." In this respect Eliphaz, Bildad and Zophar serve as unhappy examples of those whose anger had overpowered them.

Anger has been with us ever since Cain killed Abel (Genesis 4). It is triggered by one or all of the following: rejection, frustration, and humiliation. In the case of Job's friends, they probably were angered when their counsel was rejected. They then became frustrated when all their rhetoric failed to turn Job to their way of thinking; and in the end they experienced some form of inner humiliation for they were sure their logic should have persuaded him of the rightness of their cause.[63]

When Eliphaz first spoke to Job he had been courteous and tactful. Now, however, his respect for his host has evaporated like the morning mist, and he bluntly accuses Job of irreverence. Then, as an indication of the extent of his anger, he reminds him of the fate of the wicked.

Eliphaz' Renewed Attack (15:1-19)

Then Eliphaz the Temanite answered and said,

> **Should a wise man make answer with vain knowledge, and fill himself with the east wind? Should he reason with unprofitable talk, or with speeches wherewith he can do no good? Yes, you do away with fear, and hinder devotion before God. For your iniquity teaches your mouth, and you choose the speech of the crafty. Your own mouth condemns you, and not I; your own lips testify against you. Were you the first man that was born? or were you brought forth before the hills? Have you heard the secret counsel of God? And do you limit wisdom to yourself? What do you know, that we do not know? What do you understand which we do not also know? (15:2-9)**

The eminent Australian Bible scholar, Dr. Francis Andersen, whose commentary on the book of Job has been most useful, stated bluntly, "The asperity of Eliphaz'

63. For example, in 15:11 Eliphaz described his ministry of comfort as "the consolations of God"; and in 15:2-6 he censoriously accused Job of being a "windbag"who ignored the wisdom of the ages.

response indicates that he had been personally hurt" by Job's remarks.[64] By way of retaliation he accused Job of being a "bag of hot air,"[65] ignorant of the wisdom of the age, and theologically inept when it came to the sinfulness of mankind.

Because Job had been unmoved by the lengthy harangue of his friends, Eliphaz believed he might be moved by a discourse on divine judgment. And with this in mind he accused Job of irreverence (i.e., abandoning the "fear of the Lord"[66]), and indicted him for being argumentative, verbose and engaging in unprofitable rambling, and deprecating prayer (i.e., true devotion to God). Then he summed up his dismissal of Job by claiming that his defense had been faulty, and "his own lips had condemned him."

But Eliphaz was not finished. He then criticized Job for being a hypocrite, for (in his opinion) Job's protestations of innocence were nullified by his own words. His main accusation was that he set himself up against the wisdom of those who had preceded them. To try to humiliate Job he

---

64. Andersen, *Job*, 175, is most helpful. Hartley, *The Book of Job*, 242, takes a different approach. He treats this chapter as a "disputation" in which Eliphaz rejects Job's claim to wisdom (15:2-17), and provides Job with instruction about the woes of the wicked (15:17-35).
65. The wind out of the East was the searing sirocco that blew across the desert.
66. I.e., Holding God in the supreme position of Lord and walking each day in reverential awe of Him (cf. 2 Chronicles 19:7; Psalm 19:9; 111:10).

asked sarcastically if Job was the first man to be born and had he the opportunity to learn directly from communion with God so that he knew the secret counsel of the Lord? Then, showing his own pride of heart Eliphaz likened the counsel he had given Job to the "**consolations of God**."

Eliphaz' Restatement of the Doctrine of Retribution (15:20-35)

Having laid claim to the wisdom and power that emboldened him to speak on God's behalf, Eliphaz proceeded to talk about the terrible fate of the wicked. His description seems to mirror Job's present suffering with the implication that the patriarch was already suffering the torments of the damned (cf. 15:24-25:, 24:1; 27:3).

Eliphaz further states that the person in this state has no assurance that he will ever return from the realm of darkness (cf. 14:10-12), and is destined to "**fall by the sword**." Then he stated categorically that before death comes Job would wander about on the earth searching for food and living in fear that others may do him harm.

> **"The wicked man travails with pain all his days, even the number of years that are laid up for the oppressor. A sound of terrors is in his ears; in prosperity the destroyer shall come upon him. He believes that he shall not return out of darkness, and he waits for the sword. He wanders abroad for bread, saying, Where is it? He knows that the day of darkness is ready at his hand. Distress and anguish make him afraid; they prevail against him, as a king**

ready to the battle, because he has stretched out his hand against God, and behaved proudly against the Almighty ... he has lived in desolate cities, in houses which no man would inhabit, which were ready to become ruins. He shall not be rich, neither shall his substance continue. He shall not escape out of darkness; and the flame shall dry up his branches ... Let him not trust in vanity, deceiving himself; For vanity shall be his reward" (15:20-31).

And why suffer from this morbid foreboding of a painful death? Eliphaz (without proof of any kind) stated that Job had "stretched out his hand against the Almighty." He then closed his discourse with several analogies from nature, all of which point to the desperate plight of the person who neglects the way of righteousness. Finally, he sums up his counsel by saying, "There is no hope of happiness for such a person."

SOMETHING TO THINK ABOUT

Anger is something we all experience. It has been *defined* as "an intense emotional reaction, sometimes directly expressed in overt behavior and sometimes remaining a largely unexpressed feeling. It is not a disease, but rather a social event that has meaning in terms of the implicit social contract between persons."[67]

Anger has been *described* by different theorists in different ways:

> One of the most popular theories is to see anger as gradually filling a reservoir until a breach is made in the wall and the person's anger gushes out. The individual then feels much better, repairs the wall, but will repeat the same process when the pressure inside him/her becomes more than he/she can control.
>
> A second theory contends that when some event thwarts or nullifies an individual's efforts, anger may be released as aggression (either verbal or physical or both, as in the case of Cain), and the larger the gap between one's expectations and achievements, the more likely one is to become angry.
>
> A third view puts forth the theory that anger is a socially learned behavior. It is believed that the socialization of angry feelings is affected by experience and by observing others' success with aggressive behavior. Anger, therefore, is a state of arousal that can be experienced depending on how the source is perceived.

The more closely I have studied the book of Job the more I have been able to understand the persons with whom I have worked, and it is instructive to apply the approaches

67. Cf. D. G. Benner, ed., *Baker Encyclopedia of Psychology* (Grand Rapids: Baker, 1985), 58-59.

of these theorists to Job's friends. In each case it will be found that they are different, even though the common factor binding them together is one of anger.

The Bible has much to say about anger, and not all causes are the same. A concordance study will readily reveal the different kinds of situations in which anger can be either appropriate or inappropriate (cf. 1 Samuel 20:30-34; 25:5-34). And let it be noted that inappropriate anger inhibits spiritual growth.

As time permits, take a piece of paper and a pen or pencil and categorize the following select references to anger into what is appropriate or inappropriate, what causes God's anger to burn against sinners and how anger may be ameliorated: Exodus 22:24; 32:19; Deuteronomy 13:17; 1 Kings 16:13; Job 5:2; 9:13; Psalm 6:1; 30:5; Proverbs 14:29; 22:24; Isaiah 5:25; and, in the New Testament, Ephesians 4:26-27; Colossians 3:8; and James 1:19.

CHAPTER TWELVE

JOB'S RESPONSE TO ELIPHAZ' SECOND DIATRIBE

Job Feels Himself Forsaken By His Friends (16:1-5)

Eliphaz' second speech had been harsh and devoid of comfort. We are not surprised, therefore, to find Job rebuking him and the others for being "**miserable comforters**" (16:2), for Job had been deeply wounded by the callousness of those from whom he expected some measure of understanding. Eliphaz' words had left him feeling deeply hurt. He was learning the truth of the old Oriental proverb, "A tongue three inches long can kill a man six feet tall."

A careful reading of chapter 15 reveals the depth of Eliphaz' anger. He accused Job of being so lacking in intelligence that a wise man would not deign to answer his accusations. He also complained that Job had engaged in useless talk (i.e., arguments that were unprofitable). And he stated that Job was his own worst enemy, for he hindered mediation before God, and claimed that Job had used the same kind of duplicity employed by those who are devoid of the truth.

Words can be most hurtful. We've all been guilty of saying unkind things to or about others, and we have sometimes been on the receiving end of unjust slander and malicious innuendo. We do well to remember the words of James W. Foley (1874-1939), and remind ourselves about the misuse of our tongues (cf. James 3:5-12):

Drop a pebble in the water:
just a splash and it is gone;
But there's half-a-hundred ripples
circling on and on and on,
Spreading, spreading from the center,
flowing on out to the sea.
And there's no way of telling
where the end is going to be.

Drop an unkind word, or careless;
in a minute you forget;
But there's little waves a flowing,
and there's ripples circling yet,
And perhaps in some sad heart
a mighty wave of tears you've stirred,
And disturbed a life was happy
where you dropped that unkind word.

Drop a word of cheer and kindness:
in a minute you forget;
But there's gladness still a-swelling,
and there's joy a-circling yet,
And you've rolled a wave of comfort
whose sweet music can be heard
Over miles of water
just by dropping one kind word.[68]

In spite of the former blandishment of his friends, Job's despair was real. His thoughts now turned to the Lord. The Hebrew text is difficult to understand.[69] A comparison of different English translations does little to explain the biblical author's concern. Only a literal translation can adequately help us understand how Job felt. He believed that God had attacked him like a rapacious beast, that his enemies had physically abused him, and that the Lord, first like an archer and then as a swordsman, had wounded and mutilated him.

Job Feels Himself Forsaken By God (16:6–17)

Verse 6 is apparently transitional. It is evident that Job found no comfort in either the speech or the silence of his friends. He took the occasion to remind Eliphaz, Bildad and Zophar that if the present situation had been reversed he would have attempted to strengthen them as they faced their difficulties and to ease their suffering by offering words of comfort. By contrast, they had not eased his pain.

---

68. Foley's poem "Drop a Pebble in the Water" has been reprinted many times, often anonymously. Because there is no copy of Foley's poems extant, we can only presume that it is now in public domain. In regards to the biblical teaching on the use and abuse of the tongue, see James 3:5-12, and note the compilation of references in W. A. Elwell's *Topical Analysis on the Bible* (Grand Rapids: Baker, 1991), 328, col.a.
69. Cf. Clines, *Job 1–20*, 380-88; Habel, *The Book of Job,* 267-74; Hartley, *The Book of Job*, 245-47.

Here is an attempt to get at the truth of the passage in which Job, in his languid state, believed that God had also taken sides against him.

> **But now He has made me weary; You have made desolate all my company. You have laid fast hold on me ... and my leanness rises up against me, it testifies to my face. His anger has torn me and hunted me down, He has gnashed at me: my adversary glares at me. They have gaped at me with their mouth; in their contempt they have slapped me upon the cheek; they have gathered themselves together against me. God has delivered me to the ungodly, and cast me into the hands of the wicked. I was at ease, and he shattered me asunder; and he has taken me by the neck, and dashed me to pieces; He has also set me up for His mark** (i.e., as His target). **His archers surround me. He splits my kidneys open; He pours out my gall upon the ground. He breaks through me with breach upon breach; He runs at me like a warrior. I have sewn sackcloth upon my skin, and thrust my horn in the dust. My face is flushed with weeping, and on my eyelids is the shadow of death;** [He has done all this] **even though there is no violence in my hands, and my prayer is pure.** (16:7-17)

It is not difficult to imagine Job's despair. He felt he was alone and had to face irresistible force(s) without help from anyone. The false comfort of his supposed friends had had an effect upon him, and he had begun to fear that God had forsaken him. It was like a frightful nightmare in which he believed that God had become his enemy and tormentor.[70]

Finally, in desperation Job said, "**My spirit is broken, my days are extinguished, the grave is** [ready] **for me. Surely mockers are with me ...**" (17:1-2). His thoughts are crowded together in brief, jumbled sentences. He senses that death is imminent, and that the days of his life have come to an untimely end.

Then he appealed to God for vindication. (This, of course, was the exact opposite of what Satan predicted that he would do, *viz.*, "curse God and die.") Of course, Job had no means of knowing what the future held for him, and so he asked for some assurance: "**Give now a pledge, be surety for me with Yourself; who is there that will strike hands with me?**[71] **For You have hid their heart from understanding, therefore You will not exalt them.... That is why You must not let them triumph**" (17:3-4).

Job's words involve a formal handing over of his accusers/tormentors to God's tribunal. The charge is that they were mockers of his beliefs and trust in God. Though the Mosaic Law had not yet been given to God's people it is interesting to note that the penalty for malicious slander was to assign to his accusers the punishment wrongfully applied to the accused (cf. Deuteronomy 19:15-21)! In this way the entire matter was to be left in God's hands, and the really guilty party would receive his punishment from God.[72]

70. Unger, *Commentary on the Old Testament*, 700.

71. An ancient custom by which pledges were ratified by the striking of hands (Proverbs 6:1; 17:18). This practice has been explained in Z. Falk's *Hebrew Law in Bible Times* (1964).

Job's Bitter Lament (17:3-9)

It is difficult to uncover a consistent theme in verses 6-9. Job appears to be angry with himself, for by maintaining his integrity he had made matters worse. He had laid himself open to the charge of hypocrisy and enabled his mockers to find fault with him; and as a person no longer protected by God he felt himself to be in a very vulnerable position. And this had made him an easy target for his critics who were quick to try and tear him down. Note his words:

> **But He has made me a byword of the people, and I am one at whom people spit. My eye also is dim by reason of sorrow, and all my members are as a shadow. Upright men shall be astonished at this, and the innocent shall stir up himself against the godless. Yet the righteous shall hold on his way, and he who has clean hands shall grow stronger and stronger (17:6-9).**

The False Hope of Job's Friends (17:10-22)

Dr. Francis Andersen, whose depth of insight constantly amazes us, wrote: "While people with base minds may make [Job] a target of popular obloquy, with no fear of divine retribution, for such a damned soul has no claim to the protection of God, those who are on God's side [like

72. This adds a new dimension to our understanding of Romans 12:19. The benefits of handing over to the Lord retribution for injustice(s) releases the individual from harboring ill feelings towards others.

Job's supposed friends] may feel that they are helping God by treating Job as a miscreant."[73]

In the face of such virulent opposition, what can Job do? Nothing, except hold to his integrity and the rightness of his conduct before God and man.

Because Job cannot understand why the Lord has treated him in this way, he felt himself bereft of help. This is not unusual, for those who suffer from a severe illness often go through a period of emotional confusion. In his deep sorrow Job imagined that he was sewing sackcloth over his skin (a sign of deep mourning) and thrusting his "horn" (a symbol of power and pride) into the dust. He had nothing left. He had been overwhelmed by his misfortunes.[74] In the end all he could say was, "**Where then is my hope? And who regards it? Will it go down with me to the Sheol? Shall we together rest in the dust?**" (17:15-16)

In death he believed that he would finally experience rest from all his suffering. (suicide's lure)

---

73. Andersen, *Job*, 185.
74. Job acknowledged that his facial features were "flushed" (often a symptom of hepatitis), and that his suffering included impaired vision [a further evidence of leprosy].

SOMETHING TO THINK ABOUT

The great Scottish preacher, Dr. Horatius Bonar, wrote of the believer's anticipation of death:

A few more years shall roll,
A few more seasons come,
And we shall be with those that rest
Asleep with in the tomb.
Then, O my Lord, prepare
My soul for that great day;
Oh, wash me in Thy precious blood,
And take my sins away.

We have a clearer understanding of death than Job possessed. Pastors and counselors who have counseled those facing death have encountered some who were passing through the "valley of the shadow" for whom the experience contained untold terrors. A few welcomed death because their faith in Christ was real!

CHAPTER THIRTEEN

THE CORRECTION OF A MORALIST

We found in an earlier chapter that Bildad was a moralist. We also found that morality is what people turn to when their religious beliefs have over time been set aside, because they interfered with the pleasures or the profits they wanted to make. And then ultimately have been forgotten.

Bildad's Second Diatribe (18:1-21)

As a moralist Bildad was a failure. He was unable to complete the tasks a moralist faces, namely, to love the unlovely, or say "I was wrong." The debate between Eliphaz and Job had aroused his anger, and given rise to his resentment. All he could do was restate the favorite proposition of his friends, *viz.*, that destructive calamities are the portion of the wicked, and this he attempted to confirm with numerous illustrations. But he so varied his images, and so heightened the coloring of his application, that modern readers have no difficulty in realizing that he had lost all objectivity.

Bildad's second speech was nothing more than an angry attack on Job using words that were calculated to hurt his host. With cruel and unfeeling rigor, and in a tone of bitterness, he reproached Job once more (18:1-4), and then launched into a discourse on the fate of the wicked (18:5-21). Whereas Eliphaz' discourse had been gentle by compaison, Bildad was content with the ideas and showed quite clearly that he had failed to appreciate Job's thoughts because they differed from his own. Eliphaz had laid justifiable stress on the mental worries of the wicked; Bildad could only focus on the wrongdoers' outward troubles.

Bildad began his diatribe by asking,

> **"How long will you hunt for words? Consider, and afterwards we will speak. Wherefore are we counted as beasts, and are become unclean in your sight? You who tear yourself in your anger, shall the earth be forsaken for you? Or shall the rock be removed out of its place?"** (18:1-4).[75]

Bildad did not have anything new to say to Job, or any counsel that would help him. He assumed that Job was wicked, but what he stated so vehemently found no correlation with Job's real need. The Hebrew text contains the plural "*you*" when addressing Job, and is probably designed to include him with those whom he regarded as impious and unworthy of respect[76].

Verses 3 and 4 reveal Bildad's anger as well as his irrationality. However, like all moralists, he must then justify

---

75. Unger, *Old Testament Commentary*, 702, col. b. Nearly all the modern commentaries have difficulty translating 18:2, and it is evident that the translators have consulted other Semitic languages in order to find suitable synonyms. The translation of the *New American Standard Bible* seems most apropos.

his system of belief. Not being able to do so he turned on Job and blamed him for not being persuaded by his arguments. He asked sarcastically if he was so senseless that he believed the divine order was to be set aside so that he might be found righteous? And this, of course, paved the way for his discussion of the doctrine of retribution (18:5-21).

According to Bildad, the moral order, which in Bildad's eyes, Job was attempting to overturn, was as immovable as the things God had created (i.e., the earth and the hills), and in his thinking the fate of the wicked followed similar strict laws. He then provided a long list of the troubles that overtake evil men, but he apparently was unaware of the fact that the incongruent images he used undermined his basic beliefs.

> **"The light of the wicked shall be put out, and the spark of his fire shall not give light. The light shall be dark in his tent, and his lamp above him shall be put out. The steps of his strength shall be straitened, and his own counsel shall cast him down. For he is cast into a net by his own feet ....**

---

76. C. S. Lewis (1898-1963) wrote, "A world of nice people, content in their own niceness, looking no further, turned away from God, would be just as desperately in need of salvation as a miserable world." Morality does not make a Christian. It comes with the sad wisdom that accompanies old age when trust in the creeds of one's church have withered, and all that is left is outwardly correct conduct and a sense of inner emptiness.

Terrors shall make him afraid on every side, and shall chase him at his heels. His strength shall be starved (lit., hunger-bitten), **and calamity shall be ready at his side. The members of his body shall be devoured by disease, and the first-born of death shall devour his members. He shall be torn from the security of his tent in which he trusts, and he shall be marched before the king of terrors....**

His roots shall be dried up beneath, and above shall his branch be cut off. Remembrance of him shall perish from the earth, and he shall have no name in the street.... He shall have neither son nor son's son among his people, nor any survivor where he sojourned...." (18:15-19)

From the foregoing it is easy to see how Bildad conjured up all sorts of terrors that would befall the unrighteous person including famine, disease and death. He painted a grisly picture of a person's rotund form becoming emaciated, his skin becoming diseased, and his firstborn being left desolate after robbers deprived him of his wealth and security.

Of course, some of his depiction of the physical horrors he described paralleled Job's misfortunes, but what is so tragic is the fact that Bildad believed every facet of the invective that he heaped upon Job.

Job's Second Answer to Bildad (19:1-29)

> **"Then Job answered and said, How long will you vex my soul, and break me in pieces with words? These ten times[77] have you reproached me: you are not ashamed that you deal hardly with me. And be it indeed that I have erred, my error remains with me. If indeed you will magnify yourselves against me, and plead against me my reproach; know now that God has subverted me, and has compassed me with his net'" (19:1-6).**

In replying to Bildad's harsh, violent and abusive verbal assault, Job indirectly rebuked his unfeeling friend by offering a pathetic account of his condition. He contended that his sufferings were not to be ascribed to himself, but to God, who had overwhelmed him with calamities that were not of his making (19:1-6).

In light of Bildad's forceful insistence that only the unjust suffer, Job struggled to regain a right concept of God (19:7-12). He could not deny what had happened to him, but asked in effect if he could still trust the God whom he had worshiped all these years? Feeling destitute he likened his position to a city besieged by an army that was intent upon its destruction. He longed for love, and blamed God for having removed all those who were dear to him.

---

77. A Hebrew expression meaning "often" or "numerous."

"He has removed my brethren far from me, and my acquaintances are wholly estranged from me. My relatives have failed, and my intimate friends have forgotten me. Those who live in my house, and my maids, consider me for a stranger. I am a foreigner in their sight. I call to my servant, but he gives me no answer, though I implore him with my mouth. My breath is offensive to my wife, and I am loathsome to the children of my own mother. Even young children despise me; if I arise, they speak against me. All my familiar friends (i.e., associates) **abhor me, and those whom I loved have turned against me....**[78]

Have pity upon me, have pity upon me, O you my friends, for the hand of God has struck me. Why do you persecute me as God does?" (19:13-22).

Perceiving, however, that he had made no impression upon his friends, Job raised his voice and expressed his ardent desire that his words could be inscribed in a book or engraved with a stylus on stone so that they could be filled with lead (19:23-24)[79].

The process of venting his feelings has given Job some release, and with faith reborn he declared that God had not

78. Feeling that he has been deprived of his friends, he stated that those who were once dear to him have forgotten his existence, and his household servants ignore him.
79. Examples of lead being used to fill in engraved work can be be found in Kitto, *Daily Bible Illustrations*, II:89-94.

forsaken him. And this led him to state for all to hear and understand that he knew he had a Redeemer.[80]

> **"I know that my Redeemer lives, and at the last He will take His stand on the earth. Even after my skin is destroyed, yet from my flesh I shall see God; Whom I myself shall behold, and Whom my eyes will see and not another"** (19:25-27. NASB).

It is interesting to take Job's statement bit-by-bit. First, he knew that he had a Redeemer whose duty it was to redress the wrongs done to him (cf. Leviticus 25:48; Deuteronomy 19:6-12). Second, he affirmed that his Redeemer was even then alive–a flesh-and-blood reality–and not someone who would one day come into existence. Of course, this points to the preincarnate Christ, the Eternal Word, who was with God the Father before time began (cf. John 1:1-3, 14). Third, he also believed that at the end of time his Redeemer would take His stand upon the earth. And fourth, that there would be a bodily resurrection when wrongs would be righted and those who have faithfully served the Lord during their lifetime will be rewarded.

---

80. A *Goel*, "Redeemer," was "next of kin" to the person needing to be saved/redeemed from whatever calamity had befallen them. In Christian theology the term is applied to the Lord Jesus Christ who gave Himself to purchase our salvation. As far as Job was concerned, he believed that God would take upon Himself to avenge the injustices done him. For a fuller discussion, see Holloman, *Kregel Dictionary of the Bible and Theology*, 445-47.

Job's brief testament to his faith leaves open for discussion many areas of thought that progressive revelation fills in, and which, under the Spirit of God, have been elaborated upon in both the Old and New Testaments. One of these is Job's firm belief in the bodily resurrection in which he joyfully anticipated the fact that even after his death "I, even I, shall see God for myself."

And this said, Job concluded his rebuttal of Bildad with a warning to his friends (19:28-29) so that they might avoid the punishment God justly administers to the proud and arrogant who persistently scorn the truth, unjustly condemn others, and fail to show kindness to those in need.

SOMETHING TO THINK ABOUT

There are many who find fault with the closing words of this chapter. They find it hard to believe that someone living long before the time of Abraham could have such a well-defined understanding of eternal salvation. Job's words, though uttered long ago, serve to remind us of the hope that is ours when we trust in the Lord Jesus for our eternal salvation. Jesse B. Pounds (1861-1921) wrote an Easter cantata that contained the words of Job's testimony.

I know that my Redeemer lives,
And on the earth again shall stand:
I know eternal life He gives,
That grace and power are in His hand.

I know, I know that Jesus lives,
And on the earth again shall stand;
I know, I know that life He gives,
That grace and power are in His hand.

I know His promise never fails,
The Word He speaks, it cannot die
Though cruel death my flesh assails,
Yet I shall see Him by and by.

I know my mansion He prepares,
That where He is there I may be;
O wondrous thought, for me He cares,
And He at last will come for me.

CHAPTER FOURTEEN

THE INHERENT FALLACIES OF DOGMATISM

Dr. Milton Rokeach opened up for us an understanding of the dogmatic personality in his book *The Open and Closed Mind,*[81] and in the process he enlarged our understanding of the authoritarian personality. He showed how relevant and irrelevant information causes a person to react to a situation in specific ways.

The dogmatic or closed-minded person fails to discriminate between relevant and irrelevant factors. They hold their views in isolation, fail to engage in logical integration with other data, and in the final analysis tend strongly to reject and be ill-informed about belief systems other than their own. Such an individual becomes closed-minded and manifests an inflexibility when confronted with other belief systems.

Zophar provides us with a useful "case-study" of a dogmatist, especially in the opening verses of chapter 20 in which he expresses his anger at Job's concluding warning of 19:29 (cf. 20:2). And so he responded to Job: **"Therefore my troubled thoughts make me answer you .... I have heard your reproof which puts me to shame; and the spirit of my understanding makes me answer."** He then asserted **"the tri-**

81. M. Rokeach, *The Open and Closed Mind* (New York: Basic, 1960).

umphing of the wicked is short, and the joy of the godless but for a moment...."

But Zophar's own words indicate that he was a thin-skinned individual whose sensitivity dwarfed his thought processes. What he had claimed for himself was lost in the heat of his words, and he imagined that Job had insulted him by discrediting his claim to be wise (20:3). His superior attitude, in which he claimed to have worked things out based on his own reasoning powers, is shown to be false (20:4).

Zophar Defends His Belief-System (20:1-29)

To further bolster his position, Zophar provided a series of arguments that supposedly proved his point. One of these was his belief that the joy of the godless is short-lived (20:5-11).

Job had already stated that the life of all men is fleeting, whether their actions are good or bad. Zophar, however, by his avoidance of the full weight of Job's argument, contended that present experience might not be the truest measure of God's justice. He claimed that if God's judgment is slow in coming it is because He is using a person's own wickedness to bring about his downfall (20:12-18). In this brief statement Zophar stated, in his own way, the old adage that the "mills of the god's retributive justice grind slowly, but they grind exceeding fine." He admited that justice is a slow process, and though evil is like delicious food, God will cause it to sour in one's stomach so that he cannot enjoy it. He then affirmed that judgment sometimes comes when a person has attained his highest success (20:19-22).

Zophar's words also reflect the common oriental belief that neglect of the poor is the worst fault of the rich. Such neglect brings God's punishment on the greedy man who has oppressed and forsaken the poor, and seized the house he has not built. In Zophar's view such riches cannot long be retained. And because of his avarice the rich man knows no quietness within him, and he is not able to enjoy any of his possessions.

But, on closer examination, there was a weakness in Zophar's theory. His theory of justice made no allowance for the repentance of the wicked (20:23-28), and many capable writers have seen in this section a statement to the effect that Zophar's view of unrighteousness precluded the possibility of repentance for those whom he deemed to be wicked.

Zophar then used the weapons of warfare to illustrate his point which focused on the inevitable doom of the wicked (cf. 20:24-25). He boldly claimed that an unfanned fire[82] would devour Job. "**The heavens shall reveal his iniquity, And the earth shall rise up against him. The increase of his house shall depart; his goods shall flow away in the day of God's anger**" (20:27-28).

---

82. Garbage and other forms of refuse was burned outside each city. The fire burned continuously as dead animals and new garbage was thrown on to the smoldering embers (cf. Jeremiah 22:19).

Zophar concludes that such an end is **"the wicked man's portion from God, even the heritage decreed to him by God."** This closing verse (20:29) further illustrates the narrowness of Zophar's beliefs, and his speech contains no hint that the person whom he characterizes as wicked could make amends and regain the favor of the Almighty. In this respect he fails to give any evidence of compassion, and whatever god he worshiped was incapable of inspiring mercy.

Job Takes Issue With Zophar's Beliefs (21:1-34)

At the end of Zophar's discourse Job had come to the conclusion that in spite of all that had happened to him, God would vindicate him. This conclusion gave Job the assurance he needed to deal positively with Zophar's erroneous views, which can best be summarized in the form of a syllogism:

All suffering is the punishment of sin:
Job is a great sufferer:
Therefore Job is a great sinner.

Job began by appealing to his friends to bear with him as he explained his position (21:1-6), and then stated that they could mock him if they disagreed with him. And if any felt inclined to interrupt him, he suggested that they place their hand over their mouth and consider carefully what he had said before ridiculing his words[83].

But this was not all. Job felt assured that the time had now come for him to launch a counter-attack. To do this he quoted their own words and then proceeded to refute them.

A Description of the Prosperity of the Wicked (21:7-16). Job's friends had stated that sin produces suffering, but they had not elaborated on the prosperity of the wicked. In answering them Job asked why wrong-doers enjoy affluence and every evidence of good fortune? If the wicked are to be punished in this life, how can Zophar account for the many people whose lives illustrate the very opposite. They have large families, and their estates are secure. Their lives are full of joy and happiness, and their death is not a long, drawn-out, painful experience.

He then quoted what these ungodly people say to God, "**Depart from us! We do not desire the knowledge of Your ways. Who is *El Shaddai*,** (the Almighty) **that we should serve Him? And what profit do we have if we pray to Him?**"

Job also pointed out that God is sovereign in His dealings with both the righteous and the wicked. Though **few troubles overwhelm them**, the wicked practice the most presumptuous lawlessness. They have no time for God, and when destruction comes suddenly upon them, and their lamp (i.e., life is snuffed out), they go down suddenly into the grave and are soon forgotten (21:17-22).

---

83. An example of placing one's hand over his mouth in temple ritual is to be found in *Ancient Near Eastern Texts* (333) as the goddess Etana mounts heavenward on Eagles wings.

Job also refuted the belief of his friends that God stores up the iniquity of the wicked for their children. He stated that the man who is dead has no contact with those who are still alive. He also questioned, "How can the deceased know that justice has been done unless the perpetrators of wrong-doing experience it for themselves?"

Next Job asked for his friends comments on God's actions (21:23-26). His question was in two parts: (1) What is to be said for the person who dies in full health; and (2) how are we to understand the lot of the person who dies in pain and goes to his grave having never tasted (i.e., enjoyed) anything good. In the grave worms feast indiscriminately on the remains of the righteous and the unrighteous. The issue is not which one was more wicked, for God deals with each person in accordance with His sovereign will.

Though some might conclude that Job was trying to use suffering to form a "yardstick" by which people could determine ***Good vs. Evil*** in people, the fact remains that the good do not always prosper and the wicked are not always happy.

Job had found that (1) The thinking of his friends was dishonest, and (2) Their logic was only bolstered by their fallacious belief-system.

Even though Zophar had appealed for credibility to "universal knowledge" (20:4), Job could see through their reasoning, and found it to be false (21:27-34). To Zophar's claim that he had superior wisdom, Job quickly pointed out that he had not been around long enough or traveled widely enough to be able to make such a claim. His supposed knowledge of primeval law was shallow and not in keeping with everyday experience. Job then cited two situations, the one of travelers attacked by robbers with only the good being killed, and the wicked being reserved for the day of disaster; and the second of a despot who died without anyone having the courage to tell him of his evil ways. These illustrations from life contradicted what Job's friends had been asserting to be factual.

Though Job had tried hard to expose the erroneous thinking of his friends, the fact remained that they would one day be subject to God's judgment (21:30-34). This is a sobering thought!

SOMETHING TO THINK ABOUT

Job has pointed out that men–good or bad–must give an account to God for the things they have said and done while on earth. We have the benefit of progressive revelation, and so benefit from a fuller understanding of God's plan and purpose for us (cf. John 5:28; 2 Corinthians 5:10). All of this highlights the importance of our responding to what the Lord has chosen to reveal. In the present day of grace, with all that the New Testament contains, we have to make a basic and fundamental decision: Who is Jesus Christ, and what shall we do with His offer of salvation? Will we accept His pardon, or hold on to some other belief of life beyond the grave? In other words, What will we do with Jesus? An unknown author wrote:

I stood alone at the bar of God
 In the hush of the twilight dim,
And faced the question that pierced my heart:
 What shall I do with Him?
Crown'd or crucified was offered to me.
 No other choice was placed before me.

I look'd on the face so marked with tears
 That were shed in His agony;
The look in His kind eyes broke my heart,
 T'was so full of love for me.
"The Crown or the Cross" it seemed to say;
 "For or against Me, choose today."

He held out His loving hands to me,
 While He pleadingly said, "Obey!"
"Make Me your choice, for I love you so,"
 And I could not say Him nay.
Crown'd, not crucified, Thus it must be!
 No other way was open to me.

I knelt in tears at the feet of Christ,
 In the hush of the twilight dim,
And all that I was or hoped or sought,
 I surrendered it all to Him.
Crown'd. Not crucified! My heart shall know
 No king but Christ, who loves me so.

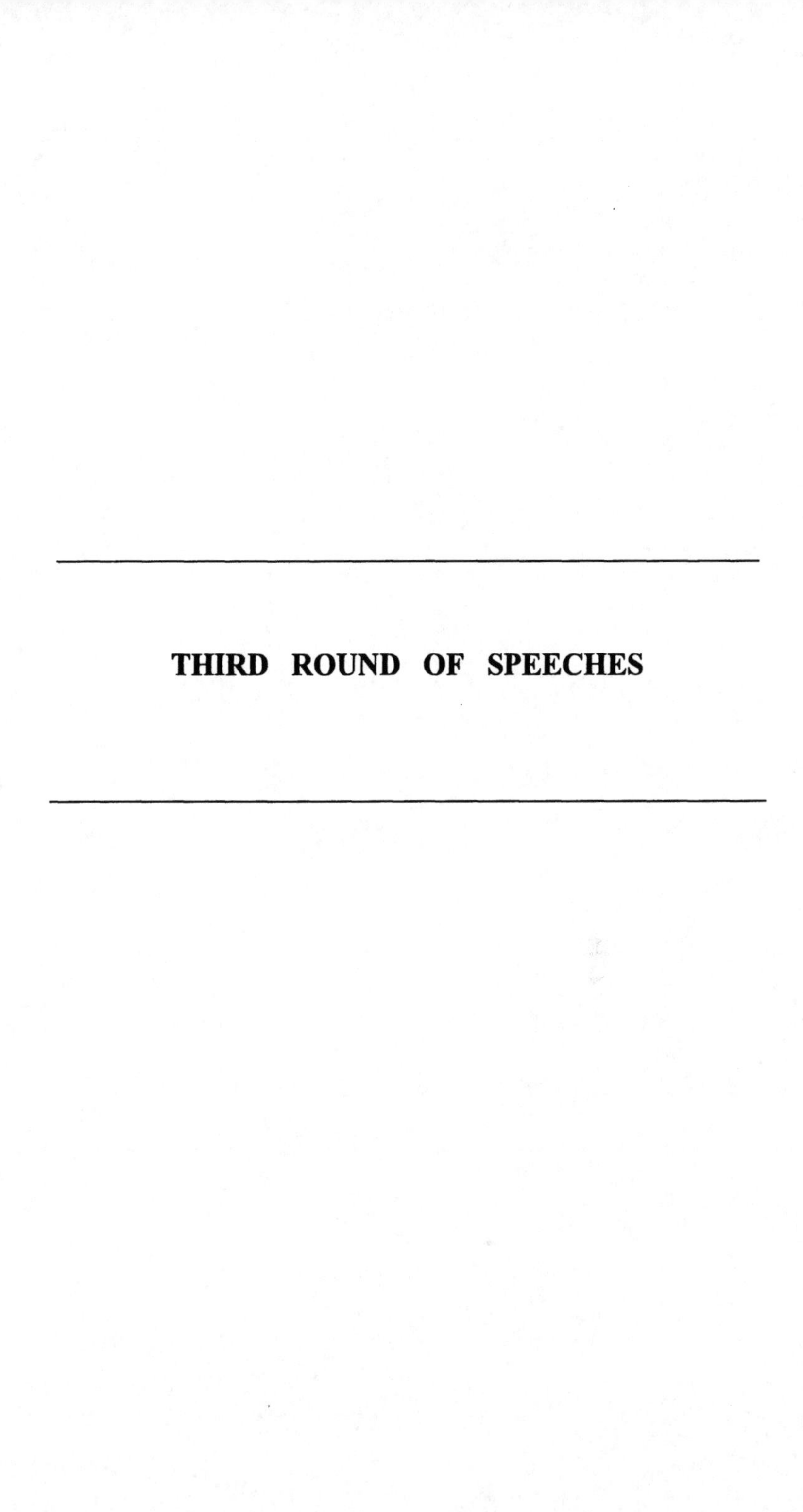

THIRD ROUND OF SPEECHES

CHAPTER FIFTEEN

JOB'S FRIENDS ARE ULTIMATELY SILENCED

We now come to the third round of speeches. Eliphaz is the first to speak. Though a good man, he comes close to losing his temper. He feels he has been unable to satisfactorily refute Job's position, and he has concluded that his friend is incorrigible and ill-disposed to consider the gravity of the charges that have been brought against him.

Each of Job's friends has shared the same erroneous presupposition (i.e., Job is suffering on account of his sins). Eliphaz, Bildad and Zophar have approached what they perceive to be Job's sinfulness and resistance to change from a different perspective. They have failed to accept their host's explanation of the problem and each one has looked at what has happened through the prism of his own mindset.

Eliphaz' Last Discourse

Chapter 22 presents its linguistic and interpretative difficulties[84], something which even the most scholarly among the intelligencia admit is baffling, and at times frustrating. We shall not take up a discussion of these difficulties because they will lead us away from the purpose of this book which is to explain as simply as possible the message of this oft neglected portion of God's Word (cf. 1 Timothy 1:5; 2 Timothy 3:16).

Previously, when twice Eliphaz had debated his friend, he had claimed that his experience enabled him to understand the reason for his friend's present suffering. When Job responded each time, he had shown how fallacious were Eliphaz' views. Finding himself in an invidious position, Eliphaz adopted a new approach, namely that Job's sin had its origin in his belief that God was morally indifferent to the conduct of the wicked.

But Eliphaz realized how tenuous was the basis of his argument and so, to support his theory, he resorted to putting words in Job's mouth. The patriarch, however, had never expressed such views. Job had never questioned God's knowledge, nor His ultimate judgment of the wicked.

It seems to us as if Eliphaz had taken the position of those who, even today, seek to discredit devout believers by twisting some of the things they may have said[85]. To do this they have cunningly devised questions that often place on the defensive the one being challenged[86].

---

84. For a discussion of the difficulties see T. Longman, III, *Job*, Baker Commentary on the Old Testament Wisdom and Psalms (Grand Rapids: Baker, 2012), 286-92. See also Habel, *Job*, 332-44, and John H. Watson, *Job*, New Application Commentary (Grand Rapids: Zondervan, 2012), 450-53.

85. We have repeated instances of this each time there is a national election, when one candidate's words about the economy are twisted and implied to his supposed indifference to the sufferings of a minority group.

Let it be noted that none of Job's supposed crimes had resulted in a single supportable charge being brought against him. No errors of omission or commission could be found in his attitude or conduct.

Eliphaz had been unable to produce any specifics in support of his criticisms, and all he could do was recount (without proof) Job's supposed indiscretions, beginning with a general statement of his extreme wickedness. He did not charge Job with dereliction in his duty toward God, but only denounced him in his treatment of others. He then appended a long list of the worse social sins (including Job's supposed failure to nourish those who were hungry and thirsty, protect the destitute, and defend of unmarried women, widows and children.)[87]

In verses 12-20 Eliphaz seems to stand in the tradition of those who believe that if they throw enough mud against a wall, some of it is sure to stick. I have worked with such individuals. They are a sorry lot, and where possible it is wise for us to keep our distance.

---

86. Note the higher ethical standards of later canonical books, *viz.*, Deuteronomy 19:15; Matthew 18:16; 2 Corinthians 13:1; and 1 Timothy 5:19. This principle is often neglected in supposedly Bible-believing circles today (cf. Hebrews 10:28)!
87. We need to remember that the laws that were to govern the life of each Israelite (e.g., The Ten Commandments with the laws concerning slaves, personal injury, theft, property damage, dishonesty, immorality, and civil and religious obligations [Exodus 22:28–23:9]) had not yet been written because Israel was several centuries removed from becoming a nation.

In trying to bolster his case he imputes to Job (without the slightest bit of evidence) the sins that brought upon the people of Noah's time the judgment of the Flood. Then, before making a final appeal to Job to repent (22:21-30), he encouraged him to receive God's Word from his mouth. This was the height of arrogance, for Eliphaz claimed to be speaking on God's behalf. While these exhortations would have been appropriate in a different context, as counsel they were inappropriate for they were not based upon Job's situation! And Eliphaz was in effect demanding that Job confess to sins he had not committed.

Eliphaz' concluding recommendation would have been apropos if Job were truly guilty. Then he promised that "**good shall come to you.... If you return to *El Shaddai*** (the Almighty), **you shall be built up**."

Bildad's Final Words

Bilhad, who gives evidence of physical and emotional exhaustion, has nothing of value to add to what has already been said (25:1-6). To avoid losing face before his friends and any who may have come to witness the proceedings on the ash heap, he pretended to be spiritual and so commented on the greatness of God. As Dr. Charles C. Ryrie has said, Bildad has run out of arguments and so does not attempt to prove Job wrong but simply declares that he is presumptuous to think he can argue with God.[88]

---

88. *Ryrie Study Bible*, (1995), 807.

"How then can man be just with God? Or how can he be clean who is born of a woman? Behold, even the moon has no brightness, and the stars are not pure in his sight: how much less man, who is a maggot (or grub)**! and the son of man, who is a worm!"** (25:4-6)

The idea is that if the heavenly bodies (for all their magnificence when reflecting the glory of the sun) are dull when compared with the glory of God, and not clean in God's sight, how can man who is abominable and corrupt reflect the splendor of heaven? He pointed out that God is all-powerful, and asserted that human righteousness pales before the glory of God.

It should be noted that Bildad did not attempt to reply to Job's argument that the righteous and the wicked alike suffer, but concluded that Job showed his lack of true piety by holding to his belief in his personal righteousness.

What of Zophar?

In bringing these discourses to a close, it should be noted that Zophar was completely silent. He had nothing to say. Most writers concede that the absence of Zophar's speech indicates that he and his friends had exhausted their attempts at rebuttal.

SOMETHING TO THINK ABOUT

Job's friends had come to him with every intention of helping him. Their motives were honorable but they failed to help or comfort him. The Apostle Paul listed "helps" among the gifts of the Holy Spirit (1 Corinthians 12:28), and so we can appropriately ask, To what extent does the discussions of Job's friends enlarge our understanding of the "gift if helps"?

One of the first things we notice is that their approach to Job's problems was almost entirely direct and (varying with the different speakers) dictatorial[89]. They had not learned how to be non-confrontational and lead by asking questions. The result of their misguided approach was that they failed to minister to Job's grief.

The harder Job's friends tried to convince him of the rightness of their opinions, the more they attempted to elevate their position over his rebuttals. The truths they derived from natural theology may have been apropos under different circumstances, but having failed to understand Job's situation, they failed to minister to his felt need.

When his friends did ask questions it was always with the intent of proving themselves right and Job wrong (cf. 22:5, 15-17). And realizing their failure, in desperation they

89. The noun *directive* has been defined as "a general instruction issued by someone in authority." To be truly helpful a person should not "lord it over" the person he/she is trying to help.

resorted to imputing to him a veritable pot-pourri of errors. This was done in the hope that they could break down his defenses and win him over to their way of thinking.

If we desire further information on the value of asking questions, all we need do is read the Gospels and note the kind of situations in which the Lord Jesus asked questions of the scribes and Pharisees, Sadducees and Herodians. And we should not overlook those who came to Him requesting a clarification of life's issues (e.g., taxes, dispersing the assets of an estate, etc.).

Job was sorely in need of consolation. His friends, however, failed to comfort him. As a result they lost their opportunity to be truly helpful. Grenville Kleiser (1868-1953), a popular American inspirational writer, penned the following well-known lines:

If I can do some good today,
If I can serve along life's way,
If I can something helpful say,
Lord, show me how.

Though there are times in our lives when we are tempted to despair, Job's experiences are of help to us. And when we are frustrated we should note how Job felt.

"Behold, I go forward but He is not there,
And backward, but I cannot perceive Him;
When He acts on the left, I cannot behold Him;
He turns on the right, I cannot see Him.
But He knows the way I take;
When He has tried me, I shall come forth as gold.

My foot has held fast to His path;
I have kept His way and not turned aside.
I have not departed from the command of His lips;
I have treasured the words of His mouth more than my necessary food. [90]

Having the same basis for trusting God in spite of our misgivings should give stability to our lives.

90. Taken from the *New American Standard Bible.*

CHAPTER SIXTEEN

HOW TO KEEP YOUR COOL

When Job's friends had come to see him they did so with the intent of being his comforters, but as these chapters show they ended up being his critics. They questioned his conduct and their censure leaves with us with the question, How much was gained by their increasingly vindictive and vociferous disapproval?

I was invited to a luncheon in honor of a man who was retiring after serving a Christian organization faithfully for many years. About twenty of his colleagues were present. Toward the end of the festivities one individual, a relative newcomer to the organization, took it upon himself to state in emphatic terms a list of the retiring individual's short-comings. His criticisms were out-of-place. If he felt so strongly about his colleagues failings, he should have shared them with him in private.

Criticisms often do more harm than good. **Cicero** (106-43 B.C.), the Roman statesman and orator, wisely observed, "It is the peculiar quality of fools to perceive the faults of others, and to forget their own." **Benjamin Disraeli** (1804-1881), Prime Minister during a particularly turbulent period of England's history, remarked, "It is much easier to be critical than to be correct." None other than **Abraham Lincoln** opined, "He has a right to criticize who has a heart to help." And **H. L. Mencken** (1880-1956)–who was a keen observer of the social mores in his day–offered the best description of the kind of advice Job's friends gave him, when he wrote: "Some people have a simple solution for every human problem, 'Neat, simplistic, and wrong.'"

The critic at the farewell luncheon failed to convince any of those present of the rightness of his views.

We have an excellent example of how to react to negative criticism in chapters 22–26 of Job's memoirs, but first we need to look over our shoulders and take note of the debate thus far. We have observed that Job's three friends had engaged in an increasingly hostile evaluation of their host's supposed shortcomings, and so a reasonable amount of review is appropriate. Initially, in what we may refer to as Round One, Job's friends had been inclined to talk in generalities about the reason for suffering, but as time went by they began attacking Job's beliefs.

In Round Two the main focus of the discussion concerned the fate of the wicked. In this exchange Job's beliefs came into open conflict with the views of his friends. Also observable was a noticeable deterioration in their relationships.

Then, in the Third Round, we found Eliphaz, who had failed to see Job's problems through Job's eyes, openly claiming that Job was self-deceived. At this stage Bildad's contribution to the debate was marginal. The brevity of his remarks reveal that he had run out of reasons to reject Job's views. He no longer attempted to prove that was Job wrong, but only stated that he was presumptuous if he thought that he could debate with God. And, of course, the trilogy would be incomplete without some word from Zophar. But where was he? He did not participate in the final round of querulous denunciation of his friend.

As we take a closer look at Job's friends we note that the needle of Bildad's gas tank was quivering on empty, whereas the gage on Zophar's dashboard indicated that his battery was flat and he was completely out of fuel.

Eliphaz' Criticism of Job (22:1-30)

In this section we find that the sheik from Teman has laid aside his gracious demeanor and donned instead the garb of a vivisectionist. He had failed to convince Job of his Godward failings and so now accused him of sins of omissions. These included taking pledges from the poor and destitute, withholding sustenance from those in dire need of food and water, abusing widows and orphans, and exploiting different situations so as to enrich himself.

All his accusations, however, were made without proof. Having made these charges, he asked in effect, "Is it any wonder that God is punishing you?" He then continued to expose what he believed to be the root cause of Job's problem, namely, his theology (22:13). He claimed that Job had failed to learn from history (22:18-19); and then added what was to him an even more grievous (though unproven) fact, namely, his belief that Job had hoarded his riches to his hurt.

Bildad's Criticism of Job (25:1-6)

Bildad had long since run out of arguments and so contented himself with vilifying Job for his presumption in thinking he could argue with the Almighty. He then attempted to discourage Job by offering "proof" from nature illustrating how impossible it was for Job to imagine that he could be pure in God's sight.

Job's Vindication of Himself (23:1–24;25; 26:1-14)[91]

Like my friend at the luncheon, Job treated the unfounded condemnation of his friends with a cool detachment. He still longed to present his case before the Lord, and struggled with the problem of the absence of God's vindication of him. He continued to believed, however, that he was a righteous man, and defiantly rejected the well-meaning but misguided counsel of his friends.

Such confidence is of encouragement to us today! Our assurance that God hears us when we petition Him reassures us that no prayer is treated by Him as trite or irrelevant.[92]

---

91. These chapters present extraordinary difficulties to the person who attempts to work from the Hebrew text. This is readily borne out as one consults different translations. Leaving aside the textual, grammatical and syntactical problems we will endeavor as best we can to explain the meaning of each passage.
92. There are some scholars who believe that 23:8-9 refers to the cardinal points of a compass. It is preferable to conclude that Job had searched for God in every direction without finding Him.

Strengthened by this belief, Job continued to struggle with the reason for his suffering, while at the same time demonstrating to his friends that he was not the defiant man they had portrayed him to be. And this led him to boldly affirm, "**He knows the way I take, and when He has tried me I shall come forth** (or possibly shine) **as gold**" (23:10).

In contrast to the harsh censorship of Eliphaz, Job could say, "**I have kept His way, and not turned aside** [from it]. **I have not gone back from the commandment of his lips,** [but] **I have treasured up the words of his mouth more than my necessary food**"(23:11-12).

When we consider that Job lived before any of the Scriptures had been written, we are amazed that he had developed such a strong Godward relationship! And he most certainly sets an example for us who have all of His inspired revelation and can meditate on all that He has chosen to reveal.

A person writing under the initials "A. M. N." had this to say:

There is a Treasure,
Rich beyond measure,
  Offered to mortals today;
Some folk despise it,
Some criticize it,
  Some would explain it away.

Some never read it,
Some never heed it,
  Some say, "It's long had it's day;"

Some people prize it,
But he who tries it
  Finds in it his comfort and stay.

Problems, however, remain. The devout believer is not exempt from them. And inasmuch as times and events are not hidden from the Almighty why does He not take issue with the ungodly and enter into judgment with them?

When we turn from 23:11-12 to 24:2-11 we note those instances in which Job exposes the crimes of the wicked. These sins included the removal of the ancient landmarks whereby one person could enlarge his own holdings while diminishing his neighbor's.[93] Such theft was directed against both the rich and the poor, and the appropriation of other people's flocks and herds apparently went along with the absorption of their land.

Plundering the property of orphans and widows was also a heinous crime. It took advantage of helpless individuals who, in a society of supposedly God-fearing people should have had special protection. Because God is omniscient as well as omnipotent Job questioned why He did not use His divine attributes and administer justice to those who oppressed the poor (24:9-12).

Next Job described those within their society who loved darkness and rebelled against the light (24:13-17). They

93. *Kudurru* were boundary markers that identified the property of a landowner.

murdered and plundered, robbed and committed adultery, and believed that because these sins were done at night no one (not even God) saw them (cf. Ezekiel 8:12). We know that inevitably a day of retribution will come, and those who have committed such sins will be punished.

But what of Bildad's comments? Though they were brief, they merit a response. Job exposed the ludicrous nature of his remarks in a series of satirical observations (26:2,3).

> **How you have helped the powerless! How you have saved the arm that has no strength! How you have counseled him who lacks wisdom, and plentifully declared sound knowledge! ...**
>
> **Those who are deceased tremble beneath the waters[94] . . . *Sheol* is naked before God and *Abaddon* has no covering. God stretches out the north over empty space, and hangs the earth upon nothing. He binds up the waters in his thick clouds; and the cloud is not torn under them. He holds back** (i.e., covers) **the face of His throne, and spreads His cloud upon it** (i.e., veils the heavens with clouds). **He has described a boundary upon the face of the waters** (and restrains their encroachment on the land) **[26:2-10].**

Job then extols the power and wisdom of God by contrasting it to Bildad's weakness and ignorance. **The pillars of heaven tremble and are astonished at His rebuke. He stirs**

94. 26:5 refers to the *repa'im*, "inhabitants of the netherworld"as trembling before the power of God. Job then speaks of *sheol* and *'abaddon* being open before God's awesome gaze.

up the sea with His power, and by His understanding He smites through Rahab (lit., "pride," but in this context perhaps referring to the power of the sea). **By His Spirit the heavens are garnished; His hand has pierced the swift, fleeing serpent. Lo, these are but the outskirts of His ways: and how small a whisper do we hear of Him! But the thunder of His power who can understand? (26:11-14).**

Had Job's friends recognized the limitations of their knowledge they would not have erred in their judgment of him. And though sorely tried, Job was able to maintain his composure in spite of their attacks.

SOMETHING TO THINK ABOUT

Ralph Spalding Cushman (1874-1960) explained how he was able to keep his cool when being vilified by his critics. He wrote:

I met God in the morning
When the day was at its best,
And His presence came like sunrise,
Like a glory in my breast.

All day long His presence lingered,
All day long He stayed with me,
And we sailed in perfect calmness
O'er a very troubled sea.

Other ships were blown and battered,
Other ships were sore distressed,
But the winds that seemed to drive them
Brought to me a peace and rest.

Then I thought of other mornings,
With a keen remorse of mind,
When I too had loosed the moorings,
With His presence left behind.

So I think I know the secret,
Learned from many a troubled way:
You must seek Him in the morning
If you want Him through the day.

Job had evidently benefitted from God's presence for many years. It had sustained him through the vicissitudes he faced when he lost his wealth, his family, and his health. There is no substitute for the assurance that comes from our confidence (or faith) in God's abiding presence with us. It sustains us no matter what difficulties block our path (cf. Psalm 139).

CHAPTER SEVENTEEN

JOB'S FINAL WORDS TO HIS FRIENDS

Some years ago a singularly brilliant churchman named John Henry Newman (1801-1890) felt that he should explain certain of his controversial actions. He did so in a book to which he gave the title, *Apologia pro Vita Sua*–A Defense of My Life. Similarly Job, in 27:1–31:40 has provided his own defense in which he explained why he held fast to his integrity and beliefs in the face of strong and unrelenting opposition from his friends.

In his final words to his friends Job commented on the fairness, impartiality and justice of God. The question he faced was how to reconcile his own misfortunes with the goodness and grace of God. Was God fair in allowing him to suffer unjustly? Calamity had struck him and his family for no apparent reason. His friends believed that God was punishing him for things that he had done that were wrong, and that only someone who had sinned greatly would suffer in this way. Job disagreed. He felt that his integrity had kept him from the enormity of the sins that his friends were attributing to him. In contrast to their belief that only the wicked suffer, he pointed out that there are many occasions when the wicked seem to prosper (12:6).

This forced Job to wrestle with additional questions: If the wicked prosper in this world, where is God's justice? And is there a reward for the righteous?

As Job looked back over his life he concluded that the seemingly easy life of the wicked is temporary, and sooner or later their actions will catch up with them (27:13-23). He also believed that those who have lived righteous lives will be blessed. His conclusion, therefore, was that God will humble the proud, and those who have walked in their integrity will be blessed (36:6; 37:23-24).

Speaking personally he affirmed that he would retain his integrity for as long as God gave him breath (27:1-23). He also reminisced on his earlier life, the charitable work that he had done, and how he believed that he could look forward to a prosperous old age. But instead of enjoying God's blessing he was now reviled by those whom he had helped. This caused him to feel completely forsaken by God. And what was very disturbing to him he also faced mounting opposition from those who disapproved of his claim that he had walked in his integrity (29:1–31:40).

Job's Determination to Maintain His Integrity (27:1-23)

Perhaps Job had paused briefly after his refutation of Bildad's short dialog to give Zophar time to respond. But when he had nothing to add, Job proceeded by speaking to all his friends,[95] and because the information that he wanted to pass on to them was of the utmost importance he prefaced his remarks with a strong oath:

> **"As God lives . . . surely my lips shall not speak unrighteously, neither shall my tongue utter deceit. Far be it**

95. The "you" of 27:11-12 is plural.

from me that I should justify you. From now and until the day I die I will not put away my integrity from me. My righteousness I hold fast, and will not let it go, [and] **my heart shall not reproach me so long as I live"** (27:2-6).

In his oath Job's dilemma becomes clear. Though he believed that God had dealt unjustly with him, he portrays for us the quandary of a righteous man who cannot disengage himself from the emotional and spiritual storm that rages in his heart.

Then, as he continued with his defense of his actions, he contrasted himself with the wicked, and named five ways in which his life was distinct from theirs: (1) He had repudiated the godless (even though this is the group in which his friends have classified him); (2) He believed that when God takes away the life of the wicked, they have no hope; (3) He had observed that when the wicked find themselves beset by trouble they have no communication with God, whereas Job believed that he has a mediator between himself and the Most High; (4) Job also believed that the wicked have no delight in fellowship with God, and only call on Him in times of trouble; and, (5) The wicked cannot teach others about God because they do not know Him, whereas Job is ready and able to teach his friends about God's ways.

Then, in an extended section, Job agreed with his friends that the destiny of the wicked involves their punishment, whereas he believed that his end would be far better than theirs (27:13-23).

Job's Poem Concerning Wisdom (28:1-28)

The material in this chapter is somewhat enigmatic, for though it stands complete in itself, it does not flow smoothly from the contents of chapter 27, nor does it blend in with the following material. Yet it does *not* leave us with the impression that it is out-of-place and should be placed elsewhere. It concerns wisdom, treating first the achievements of mankind (28:1-11), and then the wisdom of God Almighty (28:12-27).

Initially Job focused attention on man's ability to mine precious metals and valuable stones from within the earth. His description of the way in which miners extract silver, gold, and copper is most interesting. These seekers of wealth sink shafts deep into the earth and are lowered into the darkness in baskets or cages where they sway back and forth as they work away at the rock and seek to separate the valuable minerals and/or precious stones from the places where they are embedded.

As important as it is for Job's friends to be reminded of the extent of mankind's wisdom, it is even more important for them to grasp true wisdom which is referred to as the "fear (i.e., reverential awe) of the Lord," and to obey Him.[96] But where is this wisdom to be found? The value of this wisdom is far above anything that can be mined from the

---

96. God's wisdom comes only from above. The "fear of the Lord" can best be described as reverence for God, living daily in awe of Him, and having a profound respect for Him that is evidenced by a willing submission to Him.

earth. The abode of the deceased has only heard a rumor of the existence of such wisdom, for God Himself is the source of such all-encompassing understanding. Job suggests that this wisdom is to be found in God's exercise of His attributes (28:23-28).

Though people surpass animals in knowing the place of certain metals and the value of precious gems, God alone is the creator and source of wisdom.

Job's Resume of His Former Life (29:1-31:40)

In this section Job reminisce about his former happy life (29:1-10), his charities (29:11-17), his expectation of living out his life in prosperity and in the end dying the death of a respected patriarch (29:18-20). He misses his family and longs for the return of the happy days he once enjoyed.

"But now" introduces Job's lament. He cannot dwell on the honors he expected his contemporaries to pay him at death without reflecting on his present suffering (30:1-31) at the hands of those whom he had formerly helped (30:1-15). The young people, whose fathers Job would have disdained to put with his dogs, mock him and his present condition leaves him feeling humiliated. He laments what he believes to be the fact that God has forsaken him (30:16-23), and he is bewildered as he contemplates the cause of his present condition (30:24-31).

Finally, Job protests his innocence (31:1-40). His oath contains curses in which he invites God to punish him if He finds him guilty of any infraction. He is very sincere in inviting God's chastisement and lists the kind of sins of which he might be guilty, but which in point of fact cannot be lodged against him. These include sins of lust, falsehood, covetousness, adultery, injustice, the mistreatment of his servants, hardness of heart including a lack of concern for the poor, idolatry (including the worship of heavenly bodies), malice, bigotry, hypocrisy, and murder/robbery--all of which find no place in his life.

It is interesting to note that in this sweeping inventory of his inner life he begins with lust, for he is well aware of the power of one's sexual desires with the heart following one's eyes, and finally allowing oneself to be enticed by a woman into having sexual intercourse with her.

Job, however, still has his accusers. Though he had consistently maintained his integrity, modern scholars accuse him of the sin of self-righteousness.

And with these words Job ends his defense (i.e., *apologia*) of his life and conduct (31:40c).

SOMETHING TO THINK ABOUT

William Ernest Henley (1849-1903), the outspoken poet and social critic who gave us Invectus and several other literary works, also lived a life that was the antithesis of the example Job set for us. In contrast to Job, Henley did not believe in God. His confidence was in himself and in his ability to overcome whatever vicissitudes he encountered. He wrote:

Out of the night that covers me,
Black as the Pit from pole to pole,
I thank whatever gods may be
For my unconquerable soul.

In the fell clutch of circumstance
I have not winced or cried aloud.
Under the bludgeonings of chance
My head is bloody, but unbowed.

Beyond this place of wrath and tears
Looms but the Horror of the shade,[97]
And yet the menace of the years
Finds, and shall find me unafraid.

It matters not how strait the gate,
How charged with punishment the scroll,
I am the master of my fate:
I am the captain of my soul.

As a pastor I have spent many hours visiting with those who believed their life was ebbing away. Of course, they did not know precisely when they would "cross the bar" (to use Tennyson's phrase), but they felt that, as believers in the Lord Jesus Christ, they would soon see Him in all His glory.

---

97. I.e., the grave.

Some anticipated meeting Christ with a mixture of humility and confidence, while others were fearful.

Dr. Edward Musgrave Blaiklock, the renowned Professor of classics, Auckland University, Australia, summed up these chapters in the following way. "This bright flashback to the days of rest and joy" were marred by the recollection of those whom he (Job) had helped, but who now turned on him in scorn and no longer paid him his rightful measure of respect. Their conduct dishonored the aged patriarch in a contemptible manner.

Dr. Blaiklock continued: "It is a sad picture with which we leave Job–an aging man who expected to die in peace and who cannot understand why this catastrophe has overtaken him."[98]

But this is not the end. There's more to come. The best is yet to be.

98. Blaiklock, *Bible Characters*, 309.

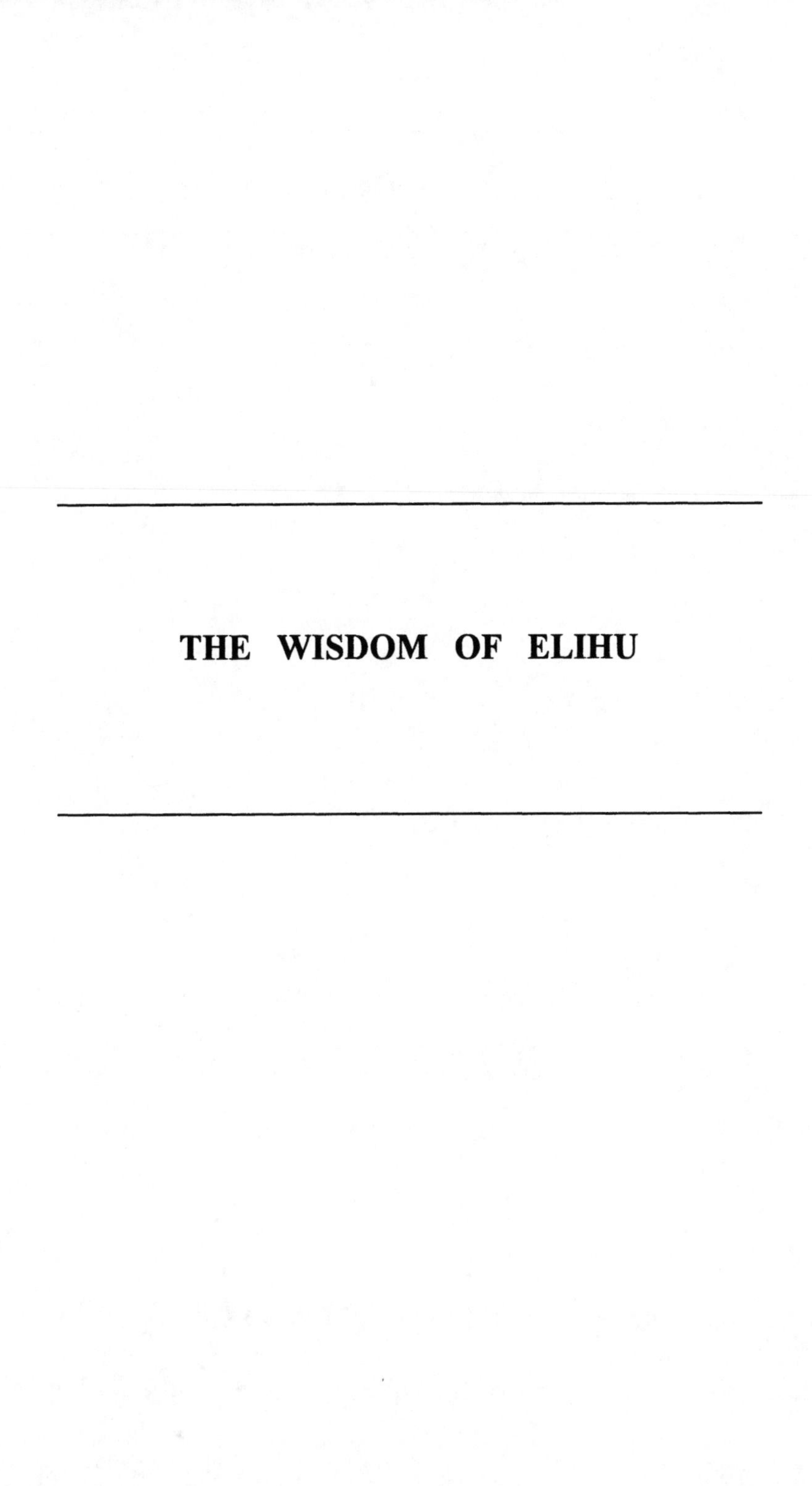

THE WISDOM OF ELIHU

CHAPTER EIGHTEEN

ELIHU'S ADVICE TO JOB

PART ONE

Elihu, whose name means "God is Yahweh," or "my God is Yahweh," was the son of Barachel. His father's name means "God blesses" and seems to point to the gratitude of his family as they thanked God for His blessings. The family to which Elihu belonged lived in Buz, a region of the Arabian Desert (cf. Jeremiah 25:23), where they apparently had earned a reputation for their piety having separated themselves from idolatry.

Elihu, though younger than Eliphaz, Bildad and Zophar, is brought before the readers of this book as a solver of problems. **So these three men** (i.e., Job's friends) **ceased to answer Job, because he was righteous in his own eyes. Then the anger of Elihu the son of Barachel the Buzite, of the family of Ram, was kindled, against Job was his anger burned, because he justified himself rather than God. And his anger burned against Job's three friends, because they had found no answer and yet had condemned Job. Now Elihu had waited to speak to Job, because (Job's three friends) were older than he. And when Elihu saw that there was no answer in the mouth of the three men, he became very angry** (32:1-5).

Finding there was no answer to Job's last speech, Elihu emerged from the shadows and, with considerable modesty (which he lost as he proceeded), commented on the discussion before delivering his own opinion on the points raised by Job's friends. He readily admitted his own anger (cf. 32:2, 3, 5), and was particularly provoked over the fact that Job's friends had condemned the patriarch without proof (cf. 32:3). He then volunteered his opinion that Job's problem was his spiritual pride, and his words touch on (although they do not thoroughly handle) the idea of the disciplinary nature of suffering, which he believed was the key to Job's perplexity and doubt.

Elihu was incensed over Job's justification of himself rather than acknowledging God's sovereignty. He, therefore, attempted to furnish a partial answer to the question of why the righteous suffer and, unwittingly, prepared the way for the answer the Lord Himself would give at the end of the book–an answer that preceded the restoration of Job to a position of blessing.

In 32:6-14 Elihu gives his reason for refraining from sharing his views sooner. He felt that a person who has lived many days and has a multitude of years (i.e., amassed considerable experience) should be in a position to teach wisdom. In the case of Job's friends, however, Elihu was disappointed. Those who appeared to be sages lacked the ability to comprehend spiritual wisdom.

All of this, Elihu said, had contributed to his own view of why Job's friends were silenced by Job's logic (32:15-22). So great was his (Elihu's) disdain for them that he did not hesitate to describe them as dismayed by Job's use of natural theology and quite unable to answer their host. Elihu had also observed that in the end they were bereft of words, and this prompted him to express his thoughts in a clear and unambiguous way so as to reduce the inner tension that had been mounting within him.

Elihu determined to express his beliefs in an honest and impartial way, without flattering anyone. This begged the question: Did Elihu believe that Job's friends had been too deferential and polite in the way they spoke to Job, or was he preparing the way for his own forthright statements?

In 33:1-4 we take note of the dignity and respect with which he treated Job, and yet he did not flinch from stating what he believed to be the truth. In this vein he challenged Job to listen to what he had to say, for there was no need for Job to fear him (33:7).

He then denounced Job's charges against God (33:8-18). He had heard Job say, **"I am clean, without transgression; I am innocent, neither is there iniquity in me."** Although his host was a good man, his notion of personal righteousness had contributed to what Elihu perceived to be spiritual pride. And this had resulted in Job taking issue with God and accusing Him of being a persecutor, and of not answering any of his prayers (33:10-12).

Elihu refuted Job's charges. He denied that God was a persecutor, and stated that God speaks to people in one of two ways: (1) in dreams and/or visions in the night, or (2) through sickness and pain (33:15-28). He then explained what dreams and visions are designed to accomplish (i.e., keeping the individual back from the kind of action or actions that would result in death and corruption). He also explained how God communicates through sickness and pain. People are often chastened by physical affliction and some even suffer from a loss of appetite.

Elihu then spoke of a mediator (33:23), a messenger from God, who may lead the inquiring individual to a sincere confession of his sin; and then stated his belief that God had found a ransom (*koper*) for him. A koper is literally a covering of sin in the sight of an infinitely holy God.

This was an aspect of God's grace and mercy that had been totally overlooked by Job's three friends.

Elihu then, in 33:24-30, described the results that follow a right response to the offer of pardon from a gracious, loving God. His/her body is spared physical death; the sufferer is restored to physical health; and he/she enjoys vital fellowship with God through prayer while luxuriating in the peace and joy of God's blessing.

Finally, Elihu encouraged Job with the knowledge that these manifestations of God's grace demonstrate His love for him. All of this was designed to show Job how deeply he had wronged his Creator by charging Him with unjustly disciplining him.

Then, as Elihu brought his first speech to a conclusion, he asked Job to be silent and heed his continuing admonition . . . unless, of course, Job wished to reply to any of the specifics Elihu had outlined. He said to Job, **"Hold your peace, and I will teach you wisdom"** (33:33).

He then went on to point out that God is not unjust (34:1-37). He quoted what he believed to be the essence of

Job's complaints (e,g., **"Job has said, 'I am righteous, and God has taken away my right.'"** But Elihu did not believe that Job was innocent because it was reported that he had gone "**in company with the workers of iniquity, and walked with wicked men...**" Where they went and what they did is left unexplained.

Furthermore, Job had been quoted as saying "**It profits a man nothing that he should delight himself with God**" (34:5, 8-9). This statement Elihu refuted. Job might claim that God had been unfair in His dealings with him, but because God is the Almighty and impartial, man reaps what he has sown, and injustice on His part would result in a reign of worldwide lawlessness. Elihu also claimed that God's **"eyes are upon the ways of a man, and He sees all he does."** His omniscience prevents injustice on His part. Instead of being unjust, His righteousness rules out any thought of compromise on His part and forms the basis of His rule over nations and individuals.

But where does all this leave you and me?

SOMETHING TO THINK ABOUT

Spiritual pride and humility may be said to be on opposite ends of a continuum. Pride is foundational to our fallen, sinful nature, and lies at the root of every type of sin (1 John 2:16). The proud person believes that he/she is better than other people (Romans 12:3), but they are unfaithful to the Lord, unthankful, insolent and arrogant (2 Chronicles 26:16;

32:25; Proverbs 21:24). They are always dissatisfied (Habakkuk 2:9), oppose God and His plans, foment strife, and seek to advance themselves by evil means. They are self-deceived and misjudge others.[99]

True humility is based on an honest self-evaluation of oneself before God, and full and complete dependence on and subject to His authority. Humility is opposed to pride and arrogance of themselves, and seek in every way to walk humbly before God.[100] Humility is necessary for salvation and spiritual growth, and the Lord Jesus is the supreme model of true humility (Phil. 2:5-8).

An unknown author expressed his/her own experience of spiritual growth in a poem entitled "Lean On Me."

"Is there no other way, O God,
  Except through sorrow, pain and loss
To stamp Christ's image on my soul?
  No other way except the Cross?

And then a voice stills all my soul,
  As stilled the waves on Galilee;
'Canst thou not bear the furnace heat,
  If 'mid the flames I walk with thee?

---

99. Holloman, *Kregel Dictionary of the Bible and Theology*, 417-19; L. O. Richards, *Expository Dictionary of Bible Words* (Grand Rapids: Regency, 1985), 346-48.

100. Holloman, 220.

'I bore the Cross, I know its weight,
  I drank the cup I hold for thee;
Canst thou not follow where I lead?
  I'll give the strength–lean thou on Me.'"

CHAPTER NINETEN

ELIHU'S ADVICE TO JOB

PART TWO

Job had been sorely tried (James 5:11), and in the book that bears his name we have the opportunity to read Elihu's own interpretation of Job's complaints against God (see chs. 35–37). He asked, "Does Job really imagine that his cause is just, and that he is a righteous man?"[101]

It should be pointed out that nowhere do we find Elihu actually quoting Job's words. At best he provided what he believed to be what Job said. This leaves us questioning by what authority Elihu presumed to act as Job's judge. Furthermore, the last section of his comments is full of difficulties, and we have to decide whether Job's irreverence (according to Elihu) was due to his stupidity or outright wickedness. The former could be cured by instruction in wisdom (i.e., in the right use of the fear of the Lord), whereas the latter would be more difficult and might possibly take longer to understand. Either way, according to Elihu, Job's culpability, when measured by his suffering, would indicate the extent of his guilt.

Elihu, however, was not prepared to leave Job to sort out his own shortcomings. He had indicted Job for his sins[102] and rebellion (i.e., open disobedience to God's

---

101. Gibson, *The Book of Job*, 191.

known will), and to these he added Job's verbosity in which he had defended himself and blamed God for his condition. And so, once again Elihu called on Job to repent for speaking **"without knowledge ... without insight ... and like the wicked men with whom he had** [supposedly] **kept company."**

The words in 35:1, **"Then Elihu continued and said ..."** indicate that he had not finished his criticism of the patriarch. In verses 1-16 he rebutted two of Job's supposed questions: "What is the use of being good?" and "Why doesn't God answer prayer?" Then he voiced his belief that unanswered prayer, including even the fervent intercession of a righteous man, may go unanswered due to lack of faith and/or the emptiness of the prayer itself (35:13).[103] But Elihu was not prepared to concede that Job was a righteous man and so claimed that God had not given heed to Job's prayer because Job's arrogance excluded him from the company of the righteous.[104]

In fairness to Job it has to be admitted that Elihu often put words in Job's mouth, and recorded that in his despair Job doubted that he would ever again experience God's

---

102. Sin has been defined as "missing the mark of rightness."
103. Gibson, *Job*, 193.
104. Elihu stated that God is too lofty to be affected either by godliness or ungodliness which only affect other people. Cf. Andersen, *Job*, 258, who rightly indicts Elihu for his impertinence, thinking of himself as "perfect in knowledge" (36:4), and who "congratulates himself on having a manageable, predictable God." Job is all to often conscious of the sovereign freedom of the Lord ... [and] prays without guarantees.

goodness. Then, in 35:4-8, Elihu must have further discouraged Job by pointing to the height of the heavens and asking, in effect, "Can a man's goodness be of any profit to him?" [105] Under the deistic[106] reasoning of 35:5-8 those who hold to such a view of God claim that neither mankind's sin or righteousness can affect God, with the result that God's administration of justice is always fair.

Elihu's conclusion appears to be correct, but his presuppositions were wrong. And in 35:9-13 we note that sufferers too often confine themselves to pitiful complaining instead of sincerely entreating the Lord. **"They cry for help by reason of the power of the mighty, but none says, 'Where is God my Maker, Who gives songs in the night, Who teaches us more than the beasts of the earth, and makes us wiser than the birds of the heavens?'"** And he stated that Job should have learned from them.

Then in 36:1–37:24, he extolled the benefits of knowing God and seeking His solution to the painful reverses of life. He pointed out that God's ways are always just (even though, to us, they may be inscrutable), and that while pain is not always punitive, it may be intended by God to refine and purify us.[107]

---

105. See Holloman's article in *Kregel's Dictionary of the Bible and Theology* (2005), in which he discusses God's immanence and transcendence (p. 172) with a fuller discussion of His immanence on pp. 227-28. His explanations are lucid and accurate. Here is a work that is of the utmost value!
106. For an explanation of deism and deistic reasoning, see Holloman, 178, col. a.
107. Unger, *Commentary on the Old Testament*, 728.

Elihu was aware of the fact that he had already been long-winded, and so asked Job and those listening to him to be patient, for he still had more to say. His statement "**For I have yet somewhat to say on God's behalf**" followed by "**I will fetch my knowledge from afar, and will ascribe righteousness to my Maker,**" indicates a haughtiness and insolence that is found among young and immature people. Neither attitude fits a person for the Lord's service, even though an individual may seek to justify his/her remark by claiming that his/her "**words are not false ...**" (36:2-4)

Fortunately for us the One whom we serve is omnipotent and omniscient, and perfect in strength and understanding. He punishes the wicked while also providing justice for the afflicted. And those whom He puts down He instructs and disciplines so that they will turn from their evil ways. If they respond to His chastening He restores them to His favor and blesses them. Those who do not turn from their sinful ways He often allows to continue in their rebellion with the result that in the end their hearts become hardened (cf. Romans 1:18-32).

As we turn from habitual sinners to the righteous we note that Scripture holds fast to the fact that the Lord has a perpetual interest in the righteous and does not withdraw His eyes from them (cf. Psalms 33:18; 34:15). He instructs them through their affliction and disciplines them so that they turn away from evil. If, however, the godless continue to sin against Him their actions show that they are treasuring up wrath against the day of judgment (cf. Romans 2:5), and their hearts are being progressively hardened.

But what of the New Testament? Is the teaching of the book of Job in harmony with these canonical writings?

As we weigh what is brought before us in 36:15-16 we note that it anticipates the teaching of the New Testament. God's love is such that time and again He entices His own to come to Him and partake of the blessings of His bounty (cf. Psalm 23:5).[108]

It was easy for Elihu to eulogize God's presence and power in nature (36:24-28), and if Job had grasped the greatness and grandeur of the Lord he would have readily submitted to His Lordship. The rain and the evaporation cycle and the thunderstorm, et cetera, all bear testimony to the fact that nature is an open book recounting God's glory--with His greatness being visibly manifested in the storm (36:29–3:7). But these truths did not prevent Elihu from challenging his hearers with the question, "Can anyone understand the spreading of the clouds or the thundering of the heavens or the lightening that He disperses about Him? The thunder declares His presence, and even cattle are made aware of what is to happen by the lightening that He disperses on the earth."

Elihu then confessed that at the light of God's power his heart trembled, for it was this kind of phenomenon that reminded him of God's attributes, and caused him to realize that he is just a creature, not the Creator. Job, however, had been so sorely tried he was in danger of retaliating against

---

108. Of course, His invitations are not always accepted (cf. Matthew 22:1-14; Luke 13:18-35).

those who had been critical of him (36:17-23). With such an attitude he was overly quick to judge others (including God), and in danger of confusing God's judgment with His plan and purpose for His people. By mixing up the issues Job was placed in the invidious position of alternately condemning God and/or man (cf. 34:33). What he needed was the kind of humble submission to God's will that would open his eyes to the truth of what was happening to him.

SOMETHING TO THINK ABOUT

The great Bible teacher, Dr. G. Campbell Morgan, who died in 1945, left behind him a record of his spiritual struggles. On one occasion he wrote "If I am not enjoying this place of maintained fellowship with the Father and with Jesus Christ, when did I depart therefrom? To that point let me return, whether it be but an hour ago or years ago, and there let me surrender at whatever cost, and do whatever God requires, however irksome it appears to be."

Elihu has given us plenty to think about. He had pointed out that God's ways are consistent (37:14-24). It was common knowledge to people living in their part of the ancient Near East that the wind out of the south brought storms and the wind from the north heralded cold weather. Accepting this as axiomatic, Elihu then challenged Job to "Hearken" to what he wished to add to his foregoing, though lengthy, discussion:

O Job: Stand still, and consider the wondrous works of God. Do you know how God lays his charge upon them, and causes the lightning of His cloud to shine? Do you know the balancing of the clouds, the wondrous works of Him who is perfect in knowledge? (37:14-16).

It isn't easy to prove that there is a God, though Elihu came close. Was he trying to prove God's goodness? As we read the Bible we find that it accepts His existence (even though skeptics have found that it is difficult to disprove His existence). The problem Elihu challenged Job to resolve was, "Is your God big enough for your life, your problems, your needs, and your painful experiences? or is He too small."

And when discouragement is dumped on us by the truck load, the question is, "Is our God big enough to help us?"

When we leave God out of our reckoning, difficulties begin to daunt us, temptations triumph over us, sin seduces us, selfish desires sway us, the world warps our thinking, situations that dwarf our abilities irritate us, and unbelief undermines our faith. But when God is recognized as the One who cares for us, then difficulties are seen as opportunities to trust Him, temptations become opportunities for victory, and service becomes a delight.

James C. Wallace (1793-1841) wrote simply yet cogently of God's omni-attributes:

There is an eye that never sleeps
Beneath the wing of night;
There is an ear that never shuts
When sink the beams of light.

There is an arm that never tires
When human strength gives way;
There is a love that never fails
When earthly loves decay.

That eye is fixed on seraph throngs;
That arm upholds the sky;
That ear is filled with angel songs;
That love is throned on high.

But there's a power which man can wield
When mortal aid is vain,
That eye, that arm, that love to reach,
That listening ear to gain.

That power is prayer, which soars on high,
To Jesus on His throne,
And moves the hand that moves the world,
And brings salvation (i.e., deliverance) down.[109]

109. "There is an Eye that Never Sleeps," by James C. Wallace (1841).

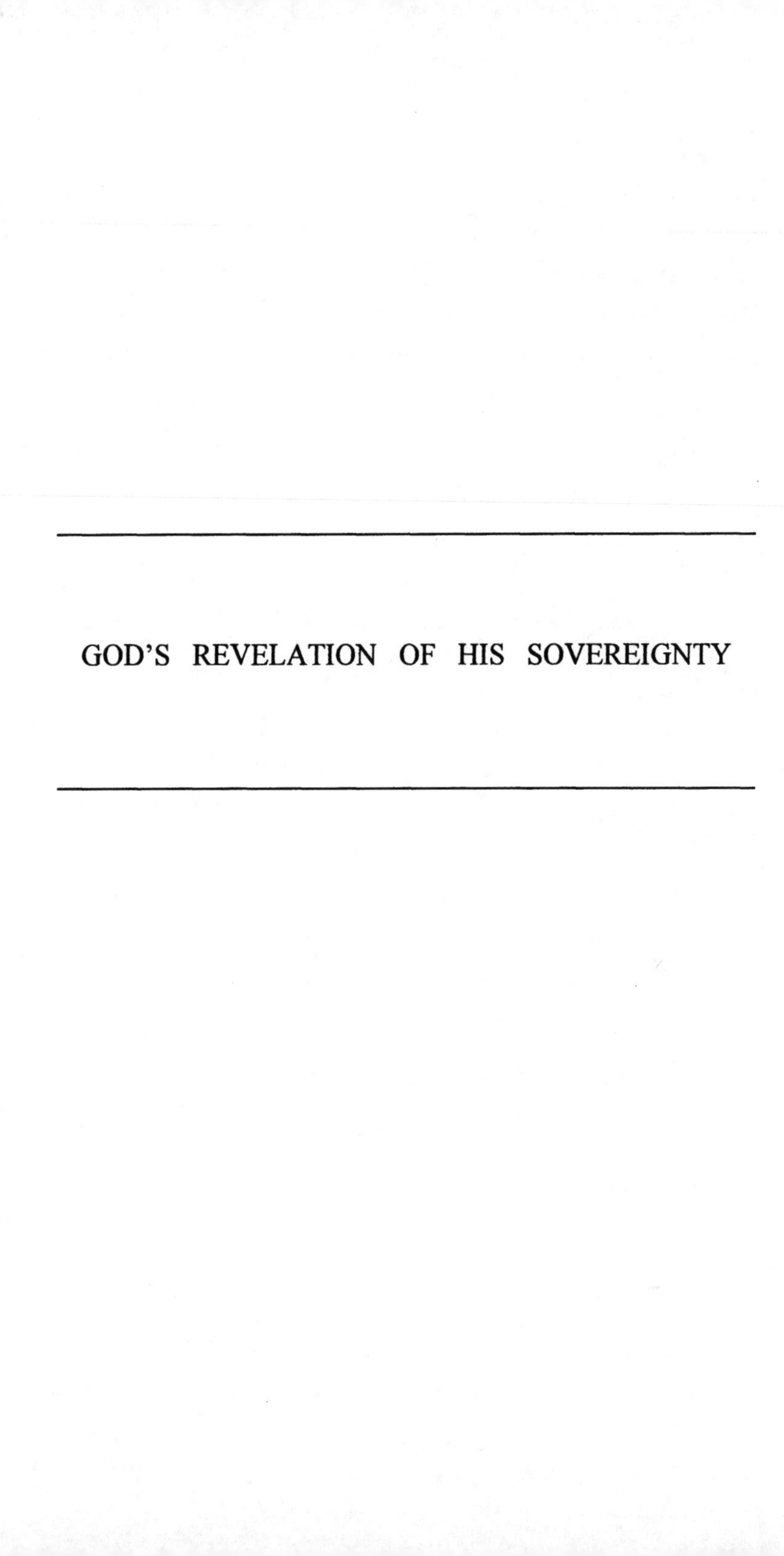

GOD'S REVELATION OF HIS SOVEREIGNTY

CHAPTER TWENTY

GOD'S REVELATION OF HIS SOVEREIGNTY PART ONE

Those sitting on the ash heap have fallen strangely silent. Eliphaz, Bildad and Zophar have found that their respective views of reality have failed to meet Job's need; and Elihu, for all of his erudition, has not spoken to Job's condition.

Off and on throughout the morning the focus of Job's friends had been on a dust cloud that had been developing in the East. Known as a sirocco, this wind brings the parched breath of the desert to scourge the entire countryside. On occasion it has been known to cause the temperature to rise steeply, perhaps as much as 16 to 22 degrees Fahrenheit above the already inhospitable desert. On such occasions the relative humidity may drop as much as 40 percent with every vestige of moisture being extracted from the air. These conditions cause those inside a house to close every door and window to preserve whatever coolness may be inside, and the East wind that brought the sirocco leaves those outside deprived of energy.[110]

---

110. D. Baly, *The Geography of the Bible*, new and rev. edition (New York: Harper & Row, 1974), 52-53; see also 64-65.

The wind which those on the ash heap had been watching had traveled swiftly, and it came upon Job and his friends with customary force. Visibility was drastically reduced and each person on the ash heap clasped his robe tightly around his body to prevent his skin from being exposed to the fine sand that acted like sandpaper.

Conversation on the ash heap having dwindled, Job's friends may have wished that they had never set out on such a quixotic course, for they had failed to convince Job of his need of repentance, and had succeeded only in alienating a formerly good friend.

It must have come as a surprise to Job and his friends when the Lord Himself finally broke the silence. Speaking out of the whirlwind He asked Job about 70 questions (38:1; 40:6). What He said to Job surprises us, for He did not deal with the specifics of the sufferer's complaint. Nor did He provide a list of Job's shortcomings or sins as his friends had done. His approach was rather an invitation for Job to investigate the known world and learn true wisdom[111]. At first glance God's questions do not seem to have anything to do with the central issue of why Job had suffered so

---

111. True wisdom is to be found in the "fear of the Lord." For a discussion of "Natural Theology", see N. L. Geisler's *Baker Encyclopedia of Christian Apologetics* (Grand Rapids: Baker, 1998), 670-74. As fascinating as Natural Theology is, it has its limitations, and in the course of time this important discipline gave way to "Biblical Theology" which is based upon divine revelation. Later on emphasis was laid on Systematic Theology, which embraces a variety of disciplines.

severely. In asking him these questions God did not intend to humiliate Job, but rather to cause him to think seriously about his challenge to his Creator (cf. 23:3-5).

God's words to Job, though not indicating the reason for his suffering, tacitly show that Job was still in good standing with his Lord. This view is further reinforced by God's invitation to Job to meet with him "like a man" (38:3).

Chapters 38:1–39:30 form a unit in which the Lord confronts Job with his competency to call Him to account for what had taken place. In 38:1-3, therefore, God accepted Job's challenge and began by asserting His rulership over the earth (38:4-7). He asked, **"Where were you when I laid the foundations of the earth? Tell Me, if you have understanding. Who determined its measures ...? Or who stretched the line upon it? On what were the foundations sunk, or who laid its corner-stone when the morning stars sang together, and all the sons of God shouted for joy?"**

In response to these questions Job was dumbfounded. He could only listen, and inwardly acknowledge the greatness of the One whom he worshiped. But let us pause for a moment. Who were or are the "morning stars"? And how do they differ from the "sons of God?" Or are they both angelic beings who witnessed the creation of the heavens and earth and celebrated God's activity with songs of praise. It seems best to identify them with angelic beings (cf. Genesis 6:2; see also 2 Peter 2:4; Jude 1:6).

Having given Job evidence of His power, the Lord then asked him if he had authority over the sea. His question

(38:8-11) is most apropos: "**Who shut up the sea with doors, when it burst forth ... and placed boundaries on it, and set [its] bars and doors, and said, 'Thus far you shall come, but no farther; and here your proud waves shall stop?'**"

The truth of this passage was forcefully impressed upon me one summer when my wife and I decided to travel north along California's Highway One to Oregon. En route we saw beautiful, golden sandy beaches as well as a variety of sea-loving mammals. Having recently read through the book of Job I was impressed with the continuous "attack" of the sea on the shoreline (38:8-11). It seemed as if one line of breakers mustered enough strength to crash against the cliffs only to fall back and retreat into the briny foam. It was then succeeded by another row of waves, and then another and another. At one time, as at the Pacific Palisades farther south, the ocean appears to have succeeded for the hills that had kept the pounding surf at bay had been undermined and a part of the cliff had fallen onto the beach. But instead of the sea claiming the land, the land kept the sea in its place, thus confirming God's appointed limits that had been established at the time of creation.

But let us return to Job. The Lord, having shown His sovereignty over the sea, now moved to ask Job about the mysteries of each new day (38:12-15). Inwardly Job had to admit that he had neither the power nor the ability to control the sun or any of the things God talked about (38:16-30).

Up to this point the Lord had shown Job things in the world which he could not hope to understand. Now, speaking with the utmost familiarity, He began talking about natural phenomena. In 38:16-18 He built upon Job's knowledge of death and the sea, and also snow, hail, wind, rain, lightning, and frost or ice. All of this convinced Job that his knowledge and power was limited, for he could not make grass to grow or cause desert flowers to bloom.

But the Lord was not finished. He instructed Job about creatures whose instinct causes them to grow to maturity, mate, give birth, learn the importance of self-preservation, and live freely far removed from mankind's ability to control them. And so the Lord asked Job "**Do you know the time when the wild goats of the rock give birth? Or can you mark when the deer calves? Can you count the months that they fulfil until their young are born?" (39:1-2).**

The Lord, having made mention of the wild goats [most likely the ibex] (39:1-4), went on to talk about the wild donkey (39:5-8), the wild ox (39:9-12), the ostriches (39:13-18), the [war] horse (39:19-25), and birds of prey (39:26-30). Except for the horse, none of them had been tamed, and yet they flourished without man's help. How did they do this? God had put wisdom (including instinct) in their innermost being and given understanding to their mind. Could Job do anything less? His abilities fell far short of the things the Almighty, in His sovereignty, had given to His creation.

The Lord also asked if Job could bind the chains of the Pleaides. A variety of myths surround the Pelaides (myths that supposedly comprise the seven daughters of Atlas and Pleione who were a part of the constellation Taurus). This constellation arose in May and set at the end of October, and was used extensively by travelers.[112]

If Job could not help the Pleaides, could he loose the chords of Orion? The constellation of Orion is referred to by the prophet Amos (5:8) and by Homer in both his *Iliad* 18:486 and 22:29, and in the *Odyssey* 5:274. Orion was one of the most beautiful of constellations, and was noted for his power and of the three primary constellations about his waist.

But what of the Bear with her satellites? Could Job guide the Bear and aid her in her nightly wandering around the heavens in search of her lost cubs?

It was as if God pointed to the vast expanse of heaven and asked Job if he had power over it (38:31-33). Job's answer was wisely one of silence.

SOMETHING TO THINK ABOUT

We now come to the importance of these chapters. What are we to learn from them? Reginald Heber (1783-1826) reminded us of God's supremacy in all things when he wrote the poem that has become a famous hymn.

---

112. See Hesiod, *Works of Days*, 383; Apollodorus, 3:10; and Diodorus Sicilus, 3:60.

Holy, Holy, Holy, Lord God Almighty!
Early in the morning our song shall rise to Thee;
Holy, Holy, Holy! Merciful and mighty!
God in Three Persons, blessed Trinity.

Holy, Holy, Holy! All the saints adore Thee,
Casting down their golden crowns
around the glassy sea;
Cherubim and seraphim falling down before Thee,
Who wert and art and evermore shall be.

Holy, Holy, Holy! Tho the darkness hide Thee,
Tho the eye of sinful man Thy glory may not see.
Only Thou art holy–there is none beside Thee
Perfect in pow'r, in love and purity.

Holy, Holy, Holy, Lord God Almighty!
All Thy works shall praise Thy name
in earth and sky and sea;
Holy, Holy, Holy, Merciful and Mighty!
God in Three Persons, blessed Trinity.

Reginald Heber died at age 43. One year later his wife gathered together 57 of his poems and, with the aid of some friends, published them in book form. It was from this collection that some of his most endearing poems became our most valued hymns.

CHAPTER TWENTY-ONE

GOD'S REVELATION OF HIS SOVEREIGNTY PART TWO

The book of Job answers, in part, the question, "What is the purpose of pain?" Is there any comfort for us in the experience of Job? Or, is our only consolation to be found in the words of William Penn (1644-1718), founder of Pennsylvania, who, when asked, "Why do Christians suffer?" replied, "No pain, no palm; no thorns, no throne; no gall, no glory; no cross, no crown."

The New Testament has a great deal to say about the trials and vicissitudes of life, and the sea of troubles through which we, as believers, must pass. We read, for example, in Romans 8:16-18 "**The Spirit Himself testifies with our spirit that we are children of God, and if children, heirs also, heirs of God and fellow heirs with Christ, if indeed we suffer with Him so that we may also be glorified with Him. For I consider that the sufferings of this present time are not worthy to be compared with the glory that is to be revealed to us**" (NASB).

In his letter to the Philippians the Apostle Paul encouraged the believers to "**conduct themselves in a manner worthy of the gospel of Christ ... standing firm in one spirit, with one mind striving together for the faith of the gospel .... For to you it has been granted for Christ's sake, not only to**

believe in Him, but also to suffer for His sake" (Philippians 1:27, 29. NASB).

And Peter echoed the same sentiments when he wrote, **"If anyone suffers as a Christian, he is not to be ashamed, but is to glorify God in this name"**[113] (1 Peter 4:16). He concluded his letter by saying, **"After you have suffered for a little while, the God of all grace, who called you to His eternal glory in Christ, will Himself perfect, confirm, strengthen and establish you"** (1 Peter 5:10).

In 38:39–39:30 the Lord continued to work in Job's heart by giving him a lesson in true humility. He did not humiliate Job but taught him by exposing his ignorance of the animal kingdom[114]. He pointed out that Job should trust Him inasmuch as lions[115] do when searching for food for themselves or their whelps (38:39-40). He also asked, **"Who prepares the raven's**[116] **meals when its young cry out to Him?** (38:41).

---

113. "Christians," i.e., "Christ's ones," or "followers of Christ."
114. Of the many books on animals in the Bible one of the most reliable and useful is G. Cansdale's *Animals of Bible Lands* (Exeter, Devon, England: Paternoster, 1970), 256pp. A work by two Danish writers, V. Moller-Christiansen and K. E. J. Jorgensen, *Encyclopedia of Bible Creatures,* ed. M. T. Heinnecken, trans. A. Unhjem (Philadelphia: Fortress, 1965), 302pp., is worth consulting, if it can be found. Cansdale's work is at once accessible and highly readable.
115. Cansdale, 105-11.
116. Cansdale, 181-84.

The Lord then asked, "**Do you know when the wild mountain goats** (possibly the ibex)[117] **give birth far from the haunts of men** (39:1a); **or have you watched the calving of the doe? Can you number the months they fulfill, the length of their gestation, and the process that marks their rapid growth before they leave their mother, never to return?**" (39:1b-4).[118]

"**While you are thinking of the ibex, think too of the wild ass** (the onager)[119] **whose speed surprises those who might happen to see him. To the onager God has given the wilderness as a home and the barren land** (salt flats ?) **for his dwelling place. He scorns the tumult of the city and does not hear the shouting of the caravan mule-drivers" (39:5-7).**

The Lord continued by stating, "**The wild ox fiercely guards its independence**". It roams the plains of Syria, and though it became the sport of kings to hunt this dangerous buffalo-like beast,[120] the question God put to Job was, "**Can you domesticate this animal so that he serves you?**" (39:9-12).

God also made the ostrich–an ungainly bird that is unable to utter intelligible sounds and cannot fly, yet is savvy enough to scorn the might of man–she which waves her wings proudly, but abandons her eggs in the earth and seems unmindful of the fact that someone may trample upon

---

117. Cansdale, 87-89.
118. Cansdale, 89-92.
119. Cansdale, 94-95.
120. Cansdale, 82-84.

them or some animal crush them (39:13-18). And even when her young hatch out of their hard shells, the ostrich treats them as if they were not hers.[121]

The Lord continued: **"Job, I'm sure you have heard the snorting of the war horse.**[122] **Have you noted how he scorns man's might? He can leap like the locust and is proud of his speed, but can you make mane like his? He is impatient for battle and appears to laugh at fear and danger. He scents battle from a great distance and rushes headlong into the contest between the opposing forces"** (39:19-25).

A final touch of irony is to be seen in God's portrayal of mankind's humiliation, for the Lord pictures both the eagle and the hawk soaring upward on thermal currents, building their nests in inaccessible places, and their young feasting on those killed in battle (39:26-30)[123].

The Almighty then asked Job, **"Can you do all this?"** His intent was to cause Job to think of his limitations. It is all a part of Job's education. God's purpose was to give him a proper perspective on the world in which he lives and His amazing handiwork. Such wisdom should instill in Job a proper humility and lead him to realize that the Lord had a purpose in his suffering.

---

121. Cansdale, 190-93.
122. Cansdale, 74-79.
123. Ibid., 142-47.

SOMETHING TO THINK ABOUT

What God revealed to Job about the natural kingdom showed the wisdom of what He had done. In the process of grappling with the evidence of natural history Job came to see the Lord as the Creator and Sustainer of all things (cf. Hebrews 1:3). He also became impressed with a realization of His perfect wisdom and power. And this, as we find as the events unfold, led him to humbly submit himself to Him as his sovereign Lord.

William Cowper drew an important distinction between knowledge and wisdom. He wrote:

Knowledge and wisdom, far from being one,
Have oft times no connection.
Knowledge dwells in heads replete with thoughts of
other men:
Wisdom in minds attentive to their own.
Knowledge is proud that he has learn'd so much;
Wisdom is humble that he knows no more.

The former leads to arrogance while the latter tends to be unassuming and modest, unobtrusive, and meek. The humble attitude is the kind the Apostle Paul wrote about in Romans 12:3.

CHAPTER TWENTY-TWO

GOD'S REVELATION OF HIS SOVEREIGNTY PART THREE

When Isaiah saw God in His glory He was sitting on His throne, "high and lifted up" (Isaiah 6:1, AV), and the train of His robe filled the Temple. It was an awesome sight, and Isaiah never forgot it.

Job did not see God in this way, for the Lord spoke to him out of the whirlwind. Job, however, never forgot what had taken place on the ash heap. The questions the Lord had asked him about the world and the animal kingdom impressed Job with God's omni-attributes[124] (38:1–39:30). This knowledge forced Job to conclude that he had spoken foolishly and that God's government of everything He had created revealed His wisdom, power and ability to order everything in the world while keeping it in perfect harmony. But this is not where Job's education ended.

Job was now meek and submissive, but he still needed to repent of his audacity. God had concluded His first speech to Job by issuing him with a challenge: **"Will the faultfinder contend with the Almighty? Let him who reproves**

124. I.e., His omniscience, omnipotence, and omnipresence.

God answer it" (40:1). **"But Job answered Yahweh and said, 'Behold, I am insignificant; what can I reply to You? I lay my hand on my mouth. Once I have spoken, and I will not answer; even twice, and I will add nothing more'"** (40:2-5).

The Lord had accused Job of charging Him with wrongdoing, and now Job responded with befitting humility. But the Lord had more to say to Job, and so He continued to speak to him out of the storm. He challenged him to face Him like a man, and then asked if Job would continue to accuse Him of injustice. To this Job was wisely silent.

Next God asked Job if he had the attributes of the Almighty (i.e., "**Do you have an arm like God's? ... Can your voice thunder like His?**"). Obviously Job lacked the power of the Lord and could not speak with His authority. God then invited Job to clothe himself with honor and majesty and see if, by such adornment, he could exercise authority and do a better job of running the universe. Then the Lord invited Job to exercise the same kind of power He possessed. Such potency could be demonstrated by humbling the proud and rebellious members of the human race and judging them for their vaunted self-righteousness.

Power Over Behemoth

In 40:15-24 God used Behemoth to illustrate His wisdom and power. He invited Job to consider this animal who was a created creature like Job. Many have disputed the identity of the Behemoth, but it is most likely that the Lord had in mind the hippopotamus[125]. Because it is a part of

God's creative activity (as was Job himself), the Lord asked Job if he had the power to trap and tame him.

The hippopotamus is a huge, odd-looking creature, which when full grown can attain a length of more than twelve feet and weigh more than a ton. The purpose behind God's reference to the hippo is to impress upon Job the fact that he has no right to demand an accounting from the Lord who can create such a marvelous creature.

The hippo was known to inhabit the Orontes River in Syria around 1500 B.C., and also was known to frequent the lower Nile in Egypt until the 12th century A.D. It was hunted with harpoons containing barbed hooks. Now it is found almost exclusively in Central Africa.

The massive head of the hippo is almost square. Its highly developed sense organs are so arranged that even when the creature is in the water its ears, eyes and nose barely break the surface. As a result it can see and hear and smell everything and hardly be noticed. Its mouth, covered by a large upper lip, is broad, yet allows for large teeth to protrude giving it a fearsome appearance when provoked.[126]

---

125. God uses a certain amount of poetic license (including hyperbole, e.g., 40:16-18) in describing Behemoth. God's point is this: "Since I made both Behemoth and you, Job, and you cannot control even this fellow creature, how dare you think of usurping My place?" (See the *Ryrie Study Bible*, 826 (note 40:15).

Power Over Leviathan

Then in 41:1-34 the Lord illustrated His greatness by asking Job if he could capture and domesticate Leviathan (generally identified as the crocodile).[127] Could this be done with a fishhook, or would Job use a cord through his nose to capture him? God anticipated Job's negative answer, and so asked if Leviathan would enter into a treaty with Job whereby he would be his slave for life? He also asked if it was possible that Leviathan could be bought and sold?

Since none of these suggestions seemed plausible, the Lord questioned if there was any way Leviathan could be captured and subdued? But even if this were possible, what use would he be? If he chose to come ashore and bask in the sun, none could rouse him; and if he were prodded into wakefulness no strategy would suffice to bring him under

---

126. In my teens I spent some time in Central and Southern Africa. I did not realize it then, but camping trips on the bank of a large tributary that flowed into the Limpopo River gave me the opportunity to observe hippos firsthand. I also watched crocodiles on the farther bank as they basked in the sun, but none were close enough for me to observe too many details about them. Over the years I have made up for this lack by watching National Geographic documentaries on television.
127. The identity of Leviathan has been disputed with some learned individuals identifying him with mythological sea monsters or sharks or one of a variety of whales or even a now extinct marine dinosaur. The most plausible explanation would seem to be the crocodile. (41:18-21 is another instance of the use of hyperbole.)

control. Furthermore, he is at home in the water where no one can corral him.

The crocodile was widely known throughout the ancient Near and Middle East, with remains dating from the Pleistocene period being found in the caves of the Mount Carmel range. In Ancient Egypt crocodiles were considered holy creatures, and were venerated as a symbol of sunrise. They were also looked upon as one of the assistants of Osiris; and in Thebes a young crocodile was kept in the temple and decorated with all sorts of jewelry.

Crocodiles are carnivorous creatures eating carrion, and feasting on whatever may be easily procured including cattle, sheep, and humans that can be captured while walking along the bank or attempting to cross the river.

SOMETHING TO THINK ABOUT

What was God's purpose in asking Job questions about nature and world?

His intent seems to have been to impress on Job His greatness and majesty, creative brilliance and superintendence of all things. There is perfection in His design and unsurpassed eminence in all that He has done.

As Job considered what the Almighty had done he realized God's supremacy in all things and his own insignificance. The only proper response to God's power was his humble submission to Him, even in matters he could not understand.

Like Job, we are limited in our abilities, and our knowledge is restricted. As we read through the Bible we realize our limitations. We like to think of ourselves as independent, but in reality we are dependent upon God for our existence as well as our food and clothing. Without God's providential care of the universe we would all die. Inasmuch as the Lord has graciously undertaken to care for us, our response to Him should be humble gratitude.

O God of earth and altar,
Bow down and hear our cry,
Our earthly rulers falter,
Our people drift and die;
Our walls of gold entomb us,
The swords of scorn divide,
Take not Thy thunder from us,
But take away our pride.[128]

128. G. K. Chesterton (1874-1936).

CHAPTER TWENTY-THREE

EPILOGUE

The story of Job's trials has come to an end. If you had been writing of his experiences how would you have "brought down the curtain" on his suffering? We are all familiar with the way Western stories end. The hero climbs onto his horse and rides off into the sunset. But that is not how the writer of these events draws to a close the events of Job's life. There are questions that must be answered before "*Finis*" can be written on the last page. And God who had spoken out of the sandstorm may want to say something to Job's friends.

Job's Repentance (42:1-6)

In these verses Job repents of his stubbornness and pride, and finds peace and contentment in the knowledge that God accepts him. He has learned that God is not only in control of the world and everything in it, but also our lives. And His love for us, which far exceeds our comprehension, is undiminished by the harsh realities of life. Note the patriarch's words:

> **Then Job answered Yahweh, and said, "I know that You can do all things, And that no purpose of Yours can be restrained. Who is this that hides counsel without knowledge? Therefore I have uttered that which I did not understand.... I have heard of You by the hearing of the ear; but now my eye sees You: wherefore I abhor myself, and repent in dust and ashes" (42:1-6).**

Job responds to the Almighty by acknowledging that He can do everything. It is an acknowledgment on his part that God is omniscient as well as omnipotent, and that man ought to be submissive. One of the goals the Lord has had in speaking to Job was to convince him of His majesty. From Job's response it is evident that He has accomplished His objective.

Job 42:3 is difficult to understand. It is evident that Job repeated what the Lord had said in 38:2. Perhaps a paraphrase of Job's words will prove helpful. It was as if Job repeated what God had said earlier, and then added: "Lord, I'm the one who spoke out-of-turn. I boldly asserted things I did not understand. I gave my opinion on subjects too profound for my limited intelligence. Now I humbly ask You, Lord, to instruct me about the things that I should know."

But Job wasn't finished. He confessed that earlier in his life he had heard about God, but now his experience with the whirlwind had given him clearer understanding[129]. God's condescension led Job to abhor himself, and repent in dust and ashes. Though he previously did not claim to be perfect, he nonetheless had an exalted conception of his own righteousness. His repentance of his pride was real, and his self-reproach was real. He likened his grief over his sinful

---

129. We are not to suppose that Job actually "saw" God. He saw the whirlwind, but there is no evidence that God appeared to Job in any visible form. He spoke from the whirlwind, but no visible manifestation of Yahweh is mentioned.

pride to humbling himself and heaping "dust and ashes" on his head.

Job's Relationships (42:7-17)

Had the book ended with 42:6 a wholly erroneous impression would have been left in our minds. Job was overwhelmed with the conviction of his guilt, and had nothing been said to his friends the impression would have been that he was wholly to blame for his illness and the calamities that had overtaken his family. It was important, therefore, that divine judgment should be pronounced on the conduct of his three friends.

Job's Friends (42:7-9). The Lord spoke to Eliphaz, who was probably the oldest, and was the one who had taken the lead in the discussions with Job. He informed him that His anger had reached the stage of being white-hot. But why was the Lord so angry with Job's friends? He explained that they had not spoken what was right about Him.

Now, God had not approved of all that Job had said, but Job's arguments tended to vindicate His character and to uphold His Lordship. When the friends had come to comfort Job and offer him their condolences, they had quickly taken on the role of his adversaries–and all in the name of the Lord Almighty.

To show their sincere repentance, Eliphaz and Bildad and Zophar were to offer sacrifices–seven bulls and seven rams. Thereafter Job would pray for them and God's wrath would be turned away from them.

Elihu was not included with Job's three friends, perhaps because his speeches to Job were nearer the truth.

Job's Family (42:10-17). The account of Job's misfortunes is coming to an end. Though Job does not know it, Satan has been shown to have misjudged him. He has suffered all that the devil's malignant wrath could heap on him. Now the Lord restores to him his former prosperity, giving him twice as much as he had before. Only the number of children remains the same as before (cf. 1:19), for Job fully expected to be reunited with those whom he had lost in the resurrection (cf. 19:26).

42:11 adds a very human touch. None of these friends and/or relatives had come to visit Job during his protracted illness. It would have added a tender touch if his "sisters" had come to empathize with him. Unhappily, when we are most in need of human comfort our friends and relatives seem to have forgotten that we even exist (cf. 19:13-14), but once Job's fortunes had been restored and he is again an influential man, they were quick to visit him.

The home of Job was again blessed with children. The Lord gave him seven sons and three daughters. His daughters are named and their beauty is attested (42:13-15). Each one was given an estate along with her brothers.

Job enjoyed considerable longevity, living for 140 years and seeing his grandsons to the fourth generation. All of this fully attested the goodness of God to him, and tacitly implied that he regained his health and virility.

SOMETHING TO THINK ABOUT

From the experiences of Job we may learn (among others) the following lessons:

- A correct view of the character and presence of God is designed to produce humility and penitence. What other Scriptures come to your mind that teach the same truth?

- A correct understanding of who God is produces in us humility (cf. Psalm 139). Job's friends had turned a deaf ear to Job's arguments, but when He revealed His will to them they willingly offered sacrifices to Him.

- In times of adversity we are all inclined to question God's goodness. This is often done in a presumptuous manner. When we give way to such irreverence, we may be tempted to criticize His handling of affairs (and believe that we could do better). The bitter experience of Job should lead us to the utmost carefulness in the manner in which we speak of our Maker.

Job ultimately came to surrender his all to the Lord, and only then did he find true peace. William Cowper suffered great emotional and physical pain, yet toward the end of his life he could write with confidence ....

God moves in a mysterious way His wonders
to perform;
He plants His footsteps in the sea and rides
upon the storm.

You fearful saints, fresh courage take:
The clouds you so much dread are big with mercy,
and shall break in blessings on your head.

Judge not the Lord by feeble sense, but trust Him
for His grace;
Behind a frowning providence faith sees a smiling face.
Blind unbelief is sure to err and scan His work in vain;
God is His own interpreter, and He will make it plain.